PENTAGON PRESS

COMMITTED TO SERVE THE ARMED FORCES

Neighbourhood Initiatives of Modi Government

Challenges and Road Ahead

Neighbourhood Initiatives of Modi Government

Challenges and Road Ahead

Editors

Prof. Nalini Kant Jha

Sreelekha K.R.

PENTAGON PRESS

Neighbourhood Initiatives of Modi Government: Challenges and Road Ahead

Editors: Prof. Nalini Kant Jha, Sreelekha K.R.

First Published in 2018

ISBN 978-93-86618-33-7

Published by

PENTAGON PRESS
206, Peacock Lane, Shahpur Jat
New Delhi-110049
Phones: 011-64706243, 26491568
Telefax: 011-26490600
email: rajan@pentagonpress.in
website: www.pentagonpress.in

Printed at Avantika Printers Private Limited.

Contents

Preface

Ever since assuming the charge of the Prime Minister, Narendra Modi has initiated transformative actions in both the fields of domestic and foreign policy. One of such initiatives in the area of foreign policy, which attracted huge domestic and global attention, is his Government's new initiatives towards India's Neighbourhood. By inviting the heads of the Governments of the South Asian countries for the swearing-in ceremony, Narendra Modi clearly indicated that improving relations with its neighbours would be a major foreign policy priority of his Government.

This proved to be true when Prime Minister Modi made his first foreign visit to Bhutan. The visit was viewed as a significant move to overhaul India's neighbourhood policy, which was in complete disarray over last some years. Both India and Bhutan reiterated their commitments to achieve the 10,000 MW target in hydropower cooperation and not to allow their territories to be used for interests inimical to each other. In the case of Nepal, the visits of Modi and Sushma Swaraj radically altered the atmospherics by making political level discourse between the two countries both pleasant and hopeful. Modi was the first Indian Prime Minister visiting Nepal in the past 17 years, who addressed the question of the trust deficit with Nepal at the political as well as public levels in that country.

As regards Bangladesh, even though the BJP had opposed the UPA II Government's move to conclude Land Boundary Agreement with Dhaka, soon after the formation of the Government, the Modi team realised the significance of friendly ties with Bangladesh in general and the benefits of the land boundary agreement in particular and hence decided to amend the Indian Constitution for implementing this agreement. In Sri Lanka, the Government soon grasped the dilemma of balancing domestic Tamil sentiments with friendly ties with Sri Lanka and did not succumb to the pressure of not inviting Sri Lankan President for the oath taking ceremony.

In Afghanistan, the Government is continuing with India's developmental assistance with Kabul and making efforts to deal with the fall-outs of the American drawdown from Afghanistan. Modi's visit to Myanmar too was intended to develop better ties with that country.

While it is too early to make an assessment of achievements of Modi Government towards improving ties with India's neighbours with a view to promote enlightened national interests, emerging trends indicate that except Pakistan, New Delhi has been able to considerably improve ties with Afghanistan, Nepal, Bangladesh, Sri Lanka and Myanmar. At the same time it was able to maintain time-tested friendship with Bhutan; with countries such as Bangladesh, Maldives and Bhutan, the Government has not been able to achieve its goal of developing very cordial ties with its neighbours.

The traditional constraints of South Asian geography, history, society, politics and role of external powers are conditioning the Government's positive moves towards its neighbours. Deep layers of suspicion and distrust cultivated through long years of the monarchy's dominance and subsequent democratic dithering in Nepal, for instance, are limiting Nepalese goodwill towards India. Nepal nationalism has been fed liberally on an anti-India diet for all these years. Politically, all the parties in Nepal are deeply divided internally owing to personality clashes and power struggles. In all these fault lines, India is a major contentious issue.

What is, however, new is that Prime Minister Modi has demonstrated his ability to shift from liberal to realist approach to respond to changing needs and circumstances in this regard. While dealing with Pakistan, for example, Modi extended an olive branch to that country by inviting Prime Minister Nawaz Sharif for the oath-taking ceremony and resuming the dialogue. But India showed the red signal when Pakistani Foreign Secretary tried to meet separatist Hurriyat leaders before talks with Indian officials. It also responded to the firing of bullets from the Pakistani side by firing mortars from the Indian side. To cap it all, New Delhi responded to Pak-sponsored terrorist attack at Uri in November 2016 by destroying several terrorist camps inside Pakistan known as 'surgical strike'; though, Islamabad denies this.

Similarly, in the case of China, he clearly told the visiting Chinese President to stop incursion of the Chinese troops into Indian territory even while welcoming him in Ahmadabad. The Government has started modernising defence preparedness such as building infrastructure on the India–China border and developing cordial ties with major powers and South-East Asian countries which have apprehensions about China. Yet, at the same time, the Modi Government is deepening economic linkages with China for India's economic advancement. Besides, taking lessons from his experience as a Chief Minister, PM Modi is recognising the role of states in promoting India's economic development.

The above outline of the Modi Government's neighbourhood initiatives raises several questions. To cite only a few: what are structural constraints that restrain India's good neighbourhood policy? What are the elements of continuity and change in India's dealing with its neighbours during the present Government? How far and to what extent the Government is moving towards serving India's national interests? What are the areas where and how the Government can do better? What policy recommendations can be made for improving India's ties with neighbours with a view to promoting national interests and larger causes of peace, security and development? How a better coordination can be achieved between the Union and States in dealing with foreign policy issues affecting particular country?

The UGC Centre for Southern Asia Studies of Pondicherry University organised a National Seminar titled "Neighbourhood Initiatives of the Modi Government: Challenges and Road Ahead", held at Pondicherry University. The present volume consists largely of papers presented during the course of the seminar.

The Essays

Jayant Prasad focused on the way Indian's foreign policy priorities are changed and emphasised the China factor and that it should be a major determinant in India's foreign policymaking process. Prof. S. D. Muni asserts that there happened a rejuvenated foreign policy course under the leadership of Prime Minister Narendra Modi, detailing India's foreign policy course towards its neighbouring states including the littoral states.

Nalini Kant Jha asserts the significance of the maritime world with regard to Indian's security and stability; from this perspective he tries to explore India's foreign policy initiatives towards Maldives under the regime of Prime Minister Narendra Modi and interestingly finds that the new regime adopted a proactive approach towards Maldives. Prof. N.K.

Jha also tried to analyse contemporary course of India's policies towards Pakistan as well. He also tried to portray strategic significance Nepal and Modi's attempt to realise its significance.

Commodore Vasan highlights challenges from the maritime world and tries to explore the Indian Ocean Region (IOR) in the sphere of security concerns of India and emphasises that India should play a proactive role to maintain stability in the region.

Venkataraman focused on Indo-Sri Lankan bilateral relations, and he stressed the need to jointly work out several issues including pending issues ranging from the fishermen issue to strategic security matters.

Anoop Kumar Gupta seeks to provide an overview of the existing policies of the Narendra Modi Government and attempts to forecast the prospective trajectories of the same. Dr Gupta has examined the foreign policy with respect to global factors and he goes on to argue the merits and demerits of neighborhood policy of Modi regime.

Sreelekha K.R. is trying to explore the ever-interesting, complicated realm in India's foreign policy, Pakistan; she tries to analyse the initial bonhomie-style diplomacy adopted by the Modi regime and its consequences and its strategic implications. Sreelekha has also attempted to analyse a significant achievement of Modi's foreign policy course towards Bangladesh; she asserts that the Modi regime won to bring both the state from proximity to closeness and cooperation.

Shivraju C.D. emphasises how geostrategic factors, economic partnership and hydropower cooperation are pertinent to a country's foreign policymaking and he tries to explore the challenges and opportunities extended by this tiny country.

Prof. Nalini Kant Jha
Sreelekha K.R.

Abbreviations

AIADMK	All India Anna Dravida Munnetra Kazhagam
ASEAN	Association of Southeast Asian Nations
ARF	ASEAN Regional Forum
BCIM	Bangladesh, China, India, Myanmar
	Bay of Bengal as Indo-Thai Coordinated Patrol
BIMSTEC	Bay of Bengal Initiative for Multi-Sectoral Technical and Economic Cooperation
BBIN	Bangladesh Bhutan Nepal India Motor Vehicle Agreement
B4B	Bharat for Bhutan
BGB	Border Guard Bangladesh
BSF	Border Security Force
CLAWS	Centre for Land Warfare Studies
CPE	China Pakistan Economic Corridor
CHOGM	Commonwealth Heads of Government Meet
CMAG	Commonwealth Ministerial Action Group
CBD	Comprehensive Bilateral Dialogue
CII	Confederation of Indian Industry
CBMP	Coordinated Border Management Plan
DQP	Dhivehi Quamee Party
DRP	Dhivehi Rayyithunge Party
EiS	Eyes in the Sky
GDP	Gross Domestic Product
GNH	Gross National Happiness'
HRA	High Risk Area
HADR	Humanitarian Aid and Disaster Relief

IOR	Indian Ocean Region
IORA	Indian Ocean Rim Association
IND-INDO CORPAT	India-Indonesia Coordinated Patrol
ICPs	Integrated Check Posts
IGMDP	Integrated Missile Development Programme
IG	Inter-governmental agreement
MARPOL	International Marine Pollution
IMBL	International Maritime Boundary Line
IMF	International Monitory Fund
ISIL	Islamic State of Iraq and Levant
JCC	Joint Consultative Commission
JWG	Joint Working Group
LBA	Land Boundary Agreement
LCSs	Land Customs Stations
LTTE	Liberation Tigers of Tamil Eelam
MNDF	Maldives National Defence Force
MSR	Maritime Silk Route
MoU	Memorandum of Understanding
MENA	Middile East and North Africa
TAR	Multi-Nation Trans-Asian Railway
NDA	National Democratic Alliance
PCA	Permanent Court of Arbitration
PIWTT	Protocol on Inland Water Transit and Trade
ReCAAP	Regional Cooperative Agreement against Armed Robbery and Piracy
SAARC	South Asian Association for Regional Cooperation
SLOCs	Sea Lanes of Communication
SIMBEX	Singapore India Maritime Bilateral Exercise
SLOCS	Source Line of Communications
SLOCS	Standard Operating Procedures
ZoP	Zone of Peace

Contributors

Jayant Prasad, IFS (Retd.)
India's Former Ambassador to Nepal & Afghanistan, Former Special Secretary, Ministry of External Affairs Government of India, currently a Visiting Fellow at the Research and Information System for Developing Countries, New Delhi, Non-Resident Fellow at the Center for the Advanced Study of India, University of Pennsylvania and Advisor at the Delhi Policy Group and currently Director General of Institute for Defence Studies and Analyses, New Delhi.

S.D. Muni
Prof. S.D. Muni, taught, conducted and supervised research in International Relations and South Asian Studies at Jawaharlal Nehru University (1974-2006), The Jawaharlal Nehru University, where he held the prestigious Appadorai Chair of International Politics and Area Studies, conferred on him the status of Professor Emeritus in 2014. Distinguished Fellow, Institute for Defence Studies & Analysis, New Delhi, India's Former Ambassador to PDR Special Envoy to Southeast Asian countries on UN Security Council Reforms.

Nalini Kant Jha
Dr Nalini Kant Jha, currently, Professor at Department of Political Science & International Studies and Director of UGC Centre for Southern Asia Studies, Pondicherry University.

D.S. Rajan
Distinguished Fellow, Chennai Centre for China Studies, Chennai; a former senior official in the Government of India. He held responsible

positions at home and abroad (Hong Kong, Tokyo and Beijing); being qualified in Chinese and Japanese languages, he also specialised in China and East Asian affairs for more than five decades.

Commodore R.S. Vasan, IN (Retd)
Currently Head Strategy and Security Studies at the Center for Asia Studies, the Director of the Chennai Centre of China Studies and the Director of the Asian Secretariat of the World Borderpol. An alumnus of the Defence Services Staff College, College of Naval Warfare (CNW) and the International Visitor Leadership Programme he has a distinguished service of over 34 years in the Indian Navy and the Coast Guard and has held prestigious command, staff and instructional appointments.

M. Venkataraman
Assistant Professor, Department of Defence and Strategic Studies, University of Madras, Chennai. His research interests are mainly on the nation state's concerns of security and foreign policy. He is also engaged as consultant, Indira Gandhi National Open University, Addis Ababa chapter, Ethiopia, Mercy Corps Ethiopia, Oromia Regional Security Bureau.

Anoop Kumar Gupta
Mr Gupta has completed his doctoral studies in international relations from Jawaharlal Nehru University, New Delhi, India. He also had been a visiting researcher at Hebrew University of Jerusalem, Israel. He is an independent scholar and freelancer.

Sreelekha K.R.
Research Fellow, UGC Centre for Southern Asia Studies, School of Social Sciences & International Studies, Pondicherry University, Pondicherry.

Shiva Raju C.D.
Junior Research Fellow, UGC Centre for Southern Asia Studies, School of Social Sciences & International Studies, Pondicherry University, Pondicherry.

1

Neighbourhood Diplomacy of Modi Government: An Overview

*Jayant Prasad**

Addressing the course of the foreign policy endeavours of the Modi Government, it is crucial to discuss what has changed and what has not changed under the new regime, especially in terms of India's perceptions on its 'neighbourhood policy'. This paper tries to mention an itemised discussion on India's relations with specific countries in the neighbourhood and explores few areas of concern with regard to India's relations with China, especially on India's reaction to Chinese President Xi Jinping's proposed 'One Belt One Road' project, in which the Maritime Silk Route is an intrinsic part. Eminent civil servant and diplomat Girija Shankar Bajpai used to define India's neighbourhood from the land stretching from the Hindukush to the Irrawaddy river and in the seas, the boundary stretch from Suez to Shangai. Pre-independence India's leaders embraced this expansive view of India's neighbourhood. Nehru's vision was reflective of this view, this outlook was reflected when he convened the Asian Relations Conference in April 1947, the conference was attended by representatives from West Asia to East and South-East Asia. The invitees had come even from China, Tibet and Iran to attend the Conference.

---

*Transcript of the lecture delivered by Jayant Prasad on the floor of a National Seminar on "Neighbourhood Initiatives of the Modi Government – Challenges and Road Ahead", organised by the UGC Centre for Southern Asia Studies, School of Social Sciences & International Studies, Pondicherry University, on April 20-22, 2015.

In the post-independence period this vision has constricted due to certain factors. The Indians were confined largely to subcontinental preoccupations. When we got independence we were among the most impoverished peoples in the world and we were preoccupied with consolidating freedom, integrating the Indian states and finally, we got embroiled in the dispute on Kashmir. Immediately after Independence, we faced a stand-off with Pakistan and a confrontation with the northern neighbour—China—that began by the mid-1950s. Consequent to this, India was geostrategically cut off from its physical continuity from the Eurasian land mass through the west, i.e. North-West Iran and Afghanistan, a situation that has lasted for nearly 68 years. India was also isolated from the north and the east because of the lack of connectivity; this, in effect was making India a landlocked state in reality. Consequently, openness to the Indian Ocean has gained an importance over time for India especially when India began integrating with the global economy since the early 1980s. Another problem faced by India with regard to its neighbourhood is that, when it comes to the cultural closeness of the subcontinent, it has had the opposite effect of reinforcing a sense of distinctiveness of India's neighbours from India. Psychological partitions of perceptions and identity have reinforced the physical fractures in South Asia.

What differentiates India's new government from the previous one is the vigour to reconnect with the nations of South Asia and the Indian Ocean region as a whole. There is a continuation of the policy but accompanied by a change of style, which is marked by greater degree of commitment to engagement with the neighbours, close contact at the level of leadership, visits to important neighbouring countries—for example, his stunning visit to Nepal, Modi's maiden visit to Bhutan—though little bit of repair work has to be done before the Bhutan visit, in order to ratify few policy options adopted by the previous regime. The previous regime seemed to have interfered in Bhutan's electoral process by cutting down assistance to some of their social programmes; it would sound better if the new Premier's visit could have repaired the damage. A mutual exchange of visits by Premiers of both India and Sri Lanka, signify their commitment to get a direct conversation with his homologous counterparts. With regard to Pakistan, a renewal of the talks has been established, though the gaps between both the states are so deep. Indians continue to underestimate the degree of paranoia in Pakistan concerning India, promoted by the Pakistan Army that insulates the Indian hand in every wrong thing that happens in Pakistan, be it a terrorist attack conducted by the Tehreek-e-Taliban or a regional disturbance in Baluchistan. For any normalisation with Pakistan, one has to start from the initiatives of the previous governments; here comes in the significance of the Shimla Agreement of 1972 and the Lahore Declaration of 1999. India has also a conundrum of determining whether Pakistan's civilian Prime Minister has the power to negotiate meaningfully with India or not and to see how far the Pakistan Army is letting him free to decide his 'India Policy'.

India's present leadership did not forget what happened to the previous BJP Prime Minister Atal Bihari Vajpayee during his visit to Pakistan in 1999. His visit was followed by the Kargil intrusion sponsored by the Pakistan Army; such a decision was the outcome of Pakistan Army's conclusion that they could overthrow the conventional status quo without inviting a reprisal from India because of the nuclear stand-off between both the countries and the nuclear parity between the two. Hence, normalisation of relations with Pakistan is bound to proceed slowly.

Except from Bhutan, India faces challenges in most countries of its neighbourhood. Bangladesh is embroiled in internal turmoil, but its relationship with India is arguably better than at any point of time prior to 1975. But, India has to deliver on some of the major promises it has made to Bangladesh, including the ratification of the land boundary agreement, the division of Teesta water and the delivery of development assistance. Afghanistan is also at a difficult transition point following the departure of the bulk of the US forces from there. Afghan President Ashraf Ghani has reversed the course by seeking Pakistan's cooperation to deal with this new situation and he is also keen to use China's help in this regard. Chinese involvement in Afghanistan is to be welcomed in the sense that, China can bring certain changes in Pakistan's position on Afghanistan; if so, it should be appreciated by India. 'To solve the Afghan issue with the cooperation of Pakistan is very difficult, but it is almost impossible to solve the Afghan issue without the cooperation of Pakistan'. Pakistanis also face problem from Afghanistan; in the past they have harboured almost a fifth of the population of Afghanistan on Pak soil, and they are still hosting about two million Afghan nationals, which is a significant proportion of the population of Afghanistan. Pakistan is also paying the price for its policies pursued towards Afghanistan; Pakistan was keen to support Islamist/Jihadist groups in Afghanistan with the support of home-grown terrorist groups, and now these groups have begun to challenge the Pakistani state itself. 'India's goodwill image' in Afghanistan is Pakistan's major conundrum; the author recollects one incident when he was a part of Track II team to visit Islamabad, then one Pakistani Air Marshal said *"Nikaah to Unka Hum Se Par Ishaq Apse Karte Hain"* it means that (wedlock is with us but there is love towards India).

In general, India's has to deal with a neighbourhood which itself is struggling hard to confront its domestic crises. For example, Nepal is still working without its promised constitution; for Sri Lanka, the issue of devolution of authority and national reconciliation has still to be attempted and Maldives is in a state of mini-crisis. Regarding our 'Look East Policy' which is now the 'Act East Policy', before endeavouring with this foreign policy practice, Prime Minister Modi has to foster connectivity with our North-Eastern states, in whose name actually the policy was launched. Apart from just pursuing the Act-East policy, India should boost investment in infrastructure and development, on which there has been no significant commitment from India towards these states, so far.

Contextualizing India's 'Neighbourhood' policy outside the framework of the South Asian subcontinent is crucial. The world is dramatically different today than from the end of the cold war. Innovation and entrepreneurship have transformed the global economic landscape. The most dramatic result of this has been China's extraordinary rise since 1979. India's Chief Economic Advisor Arvind Subramaniam wrote a book four years ago called Eclipse: Living in the Shadow of China's Economic Dominance. So enormously has grown China's economic clout that Subramaniam forecast that the Renminbi could soon replace the US Dollar as the world's reserve currency. China has already surpassed US GDP in Purchasing Power Parity terms and its economy will be twenty per cent larger than that of the US by the end of its decade. China's current foreign exchange rate reserve tops 4 trillion dollars. Its most significant achievement has been the fastest upliftment of the largest number of people in the human history in a shortest possible time out of poverty. It is quite sure that China will have a central role in shifting the nature of the world's geo-economies. Here come the significance of xi Jinping's initiatives, his 2012 vision of the Chinese dream and the 2013 vision of 'One Belt One Road', which also subsumes that the 21st century Maritime Silk Route is an intrinsic element. These are going to be important in the configuration of Eurasia and the world. Just as China wants to connect with Europe, India is already connected with the European Union; EU as a trading block constitutes India's largest trading partner both for trade in goods and trade in disembodied services. There is always speculation about the future of India-China ties and much of it is fanned by the western media. The prospects of improved relations between India and China are promising since both countries have self-assured leadership and their natural impulse will be to work together without conflict. At present there is a greater prospect for their moving forward from the scratches of the 1962 Indo-China war and the US-China entente during the Indo-Pak war in 1971. There has been no violent conflict on the Line of Actual Control for the last forty years. Although, the 1993 Agreement to maintain Peace and Tranquility and subsequent additions to it have not prevented both the parties from pushing and shudding at the border between border guards, but, they have avoided shooting at each other across the undemarcated border. China's openness on India joining the Shanghai Co-operation Organization and APEC are good signs and also China's willingness in principle to explore cooperation in areas like Afghanistan; this signifies its commitment. Chinese President Xi's visit to India in September 2014 and Indian Premier Modi's visit is expected to take place in May 2015 with hopes to take on a new momentum in the bilateral relationship between both the states. Modi has himself described that India's China policy must be pragmatic, open-minded and based on realistic expectations; India's response to China's OBOR and MSR projects are an extension of this realistic pragmatism. But there are some elements which impinge on Indian security but India has supported in principle the idea of the BCIM (Bangladesh-China-India-Myanmar) corridor which connects up to Kolkata. But India has reservations with regard to Chinese initiatives on the Pakistan-China corridor that extends from Karakoram to Gwadar, as it poses challenges to India's security concerns. For India this corridor seems illegal because India believes that the proposed corridor is passing through a piece of territory which was illegally seceded to China by Pakistan, though it is a disputed territory.

In Nepal, Chinese railways lines are coming very close to Nepal's border and there would be a possible extension of these railway connections to Kathmandu and Lumbini, down in the Terai, in the coming years, which is also a security concern for India. India could deal with these issues if we dealt with them with boldness and an inventive way. For instance, India could build the East-West railway on the alignment of the current East-West highway, mainly financed by India; the feasibility study of a such railway line has been conducted by an Indian organization named RITES. India could also promote trade from mainland China through Tibet and Nepal to India by following all the customary controls over this merchandise trade relationship. But in reality, India's north-eastern states are flooded with Chinese products which are carried by head loads, for which India does not charge any customs duties; if this could be rectified India will be benefited from this trade transaction. So India should extend constructive cooperation to those elements of the MSR where there is a consensus of benefit and interest between the two countries. These Chinese initiatives in fact aim to augment their national interest, but it is also to be noted that China is keen to transfer the resources from its surplus economy to economies which is short of investment, and for this reason, such initiatives are attractive for India. Shyam Saran, former Foreign Secretary of India, aptly noted that MSR is a Chinese orchestra, but all the countries who are participating are members of it, but the tune is Chinese and the conductor is Chinese. Thus it is essentially, a Sino-centric product; India should choose what could be embraced and what not. It is too much to expect the larger countries in Asia and Eurasia to come and board the MSR idea instantly, when it is not clear on the modalities of work and implementation mechanism. Again the idea is also facing challenges from political hostilities, asymmetries, lack of political will and traction from the local communities, etc.

China promotes its new ideas by saying that they are all about economy and development, but other countries including India find that they are also having security and strategic components. This idea is having a direct military bearing with a Chinese military presence in the South China Sea and Indian Ocean region, now which is widened up to the Mediterranean. One can say that the idea of MSR is not only derived out of geo-economics but also fostered by geostrategy and geopolitics; the moment these two latter elements are added to the international relations/ environment which became a determinant force with regard to concepts like Balance of Power, Zero Sum Game, Containment, Hedging, Divide and Rule that can subtract from the objective of President Xi of building a community of common interest.

In Asia, it is time for building a complementary effort by interested nations for crafting new security architecture and to maintain and manage common interests of cooperation in Asia including the Indian Ocean and other concerned areas. A new vision and movement should be articulated for the Asian Union with free movements of goods and services, investments, peoples, ideas and technology, etc. In conclusion, one can say that economic transformation in Asia did not produce the desired result of a more stabilised continent. To quote Hentry Kissinger's The World Order: "the world is actually in a state of relative disorder and the riots, chaos, threaten side by side with unprecedented interdependence". Indeed most great powers have turned defensive and inward-looking, besieged by anxieties that were presumed to have become forever past with the passing of the cold war. And the big three, i.e. China, Russia and the US, are restless with each of them seeking their own separate solutions to the problems that confront them. Hence, India will have to navigate its neighbourhood policy dexterously through waters that remain largely unsettled.

2

Modi's Neighbourhood Initiatives and the Road Ahead*

S.D. Muni

We are here to deliberate on the theme of Prime Minister Modi's policy towards neighbours; his initiatives and the challenges that his Government may face in the years to come. I am happy to know that the Ministry of External Affairs is co-sponsoring this Seminar. I hope that MEA officers will find time and effort to look into its deliberations. Generally, they know everything and they hardly need academics or anyone else for that matter to tell them about policy matters. The academics make their efforts and on two counts: first, to grasp and analyse how the policies unfold and secondly, at least some times, also to innovate and explore if there are new ideas to be sounded on the policymakers. It is on the second component that I wish the MEA to look into in the deliberations of this Seminar as Prof. Nalini Kant Jha has carefully tried to collect some of the best minds available.

Inherited Policy

Now coming to the theme and somewhat narrowly than done by Ambassador Jayant Prasad, let me make two or three main points before

---

* Transcript of the lecture delivered by Prof. S.D. Muni, on the floor of a National Seminar on "Neighbourhood Initiatives of the Modi Government—Challenges and Road Ahead", organised by UGC Centre for Southern Asia Studies, School of Social Sciences & International Studies, Pondicherry University, on April 20-22, 2015.

you. One, what is it which Mr Modi started with, in terms of the inheritance of the neighbourhood policy and then see how he has tried to innovate or go beyond them or change them, and lastly to look at the challenges which this policy faces. To begin with the inheritance, in terms of Mr Modi's neighbourhood policy, I think a very active neighbourhood policy did exist and for the last ten to fifteen years; even five-ten years before the UPA Government, there have been many significant changes taking place in India's neighbourhood policy. There has been a very specific push towards economic integration, particularly emphasising trade, energy and connectivity within the SAARC region. There has been a very serious effort on border management: I think it was flagged by settlement or resolution of the maritime boundary with Bangladesh; border check posts were upgraded to integrated customs check posts with Pakistan, Bangladesh and Nepal. Accordingly, various initiatives have been taken where many loose ends on the borders regarding security have been tied up. Other initiatives like the South Asian University, expansion of SAARC, where not only observers came in but new members like Afghanistan too joined. India has also played, and I am rather fond of mentioning it again and again, that India has played a very important role, almost a transformational role in the political spectrum of the neighbouring countries. In the recent years, say, last decade or so, India has facilitated, supported, helped and encouraged democratic transformation in the neighbouring countries. You see, you go ten years earlier before the beginning of this new century and you see all our neighbours littered either with monarchies or military regimes. That is no longer the reality and we have done our best to facilitate this massive change towards democratising South Asia.

Most of the initiatives or the policy moves of the previous governments were faltering on various counts. I think the first one was the delivery deficit on almost anything that India initiated or promised. There were procedural complexities, there were lack of additional financial commitments; there were also total absence of strategic and long term thinking, in terms of building neighbourhood. Then, there was also an excessive influence of various stakeholders in policymaking and policy execution. I do not say this just for raising controversies but security agencies and intelligence agencies started playing more than their due role. Their inputs were accepted without enough scrutiny leading to distorted political priorities and policy perspective. India also depended on the extra-regional powers like the United States and EU, including on the issues related to democratic transitions in Nepal, Maldives and Bhutan. India was also constrained by what China would do or would not do. There were also many instances, I hope – our diplomat colleagues would bear me out – of micro management in the day-to-day affairs of the neighbours, infuriating them and subjecting India to the charges of interference and undue pressures. This was in contrast to political indifference at the highest level. Ambassador Prasad's reference to the lack of prime ministerial visits to some of the neighbouring countries for long years is apt in this respect. There was also a very inconsistent political commitment to the forces of change and transformation which played a leading role in democratisation in the neighbouring countries concerned. Many of such forces were left high and dry before the transformational processes and institutionalisation of change could be brought to their respective conclusion. Jayant's mention of Nepal and Maldives may be recalled here. It is good, however, that in Bangladesh, we continue to stand by the progressive forces even against heavy odds. In Bhutan again we have a work-in-progress democracy which still needs to be consolidated.

In the previous policies, problems arose also because of an excessive occupation with Pakistan, which has characterised not only the neighbourhood policy of India, but the entire foreign policy from the beginning. India tried to change the course of engagement with Pakistan but failed. I must say it to the credit of Manmohan Singh's Government and to some extent the Musharraf regime in Pakistan that both of them claim that they had nearly worked out some sort of a resolution of the Kashmir problem but somehow it could not be delivered. Then India has got trapped into the terrorism tangle—the Mumbai attack of 26/11—which persists still. Now this is where broadly Modi's Government started and I think this Government started with two big advantages.

Prime Minister Modi's first advantage is that he has secured a massive mandate not available to the previous regimes. There is no coalition *Dharma* which the present Government actually has to follow in carrying out any policy, domestic or foreign. Secondly, there is a typical Gujarati DNA in Modi's way of doing things—pardon me for my regional prejudices—brought in, over which oozes entrepreneurship and adventure. That amounts to working hard and dedicatedly to do things, take initiatives, achieve success and leave an imprint on whatever you do. Modi has displayed an acute sense of history and a flair for creativity. So these are the two advantages; within these two advantages Modi's government laid down certain policy parameters.

Modi's Initiatives and Contribution

Now one policy parameter is what Mr Modi told to his top diplomats, the Heads of Missions recently in New Delhi, that India should be a "leading" not only a "balancing power". That we should not only be tinkering with the issues here and there but we must take lead and project our priorities and concerns. And within these priorities, the neighbourhood was put on top. This was evident in his invitation to the South Asian leaders for his inaugural event. Now Modi's ruling party, the Bharatiya Janata Party has defined the parameter of the foreign policy in term of five Hindi 'Sa'(s), i.e. 'Samman, Samvaad, Samridhi, Suraksha, Sabhayata and Sanskriti'. This means, dignity and self-respect, dialogue and negotiations, development and prosperity, security and defence, and culture and civilisation.

What is new in this? I find two elements are new in terms of a nuanced approach to foreign policy. One element which is new is that security has been pushed down the developmental ladder: not that the developmental ladder that did not exist in the previous government's approach to foreign policy and neighbour policies, but many times whenever the conflict came in between the developmental and the security components, in my understating, the security component was given greater attention. It remains to be seen if the new 'developmental' priority would hold in policy implementation, particularly at the time of conflict with the security concerns. The second new element is the very forceful introduction of what you call *Sabhyata and Sanskriti*, which is the soft power that has been neglected for a very long time. Some of us have been underlining this neglect in our writings and speeches. Besides these two nuances, the basic frame of policy remains the same. Modi himself has accepted that he is following the existing regime's foreign policy.

The change and Modi's imprint are more in the style and packaging policy rather than altering its basic components. Thus within this broad framework of continuity I attempt to outline and outline Modi's initiatives. To begin with, in relation to the neighbours, he has started addressing and undoing the alienation being felt among the neighbours vis-à-vis India, by infusing energy and dynamism into the policy inherited by him. This is indicated in various ways. One is the way in which he has been coining and aptly using catch phrases while reaching out to the neighbouring countries' people and political stakeholders; for instance B4B in Bhutan, *Bharat For Bhutan.* Also look at his speeches in Nepal's Constituent Assembly and Parliament of Sri Lanka, etc.

Then what has been done is the streamlining delivery mechanism in fulfilling promises made to the neighbouring countries. All of us know that he is even bypassing Ministers and working through Secretaries and lower bureaucracy to push the decisions and implementation forward. There are whispers in the Delhi's power corridors that on foreign policy, he seldom consults even his Foreign Minister. Thus we see some movements on the ground in delivering the policy and keeping the promises. The Prime Minister has a habit of fixing deadlines for concrete movement in decisions. The cases of hydropower projects in Nepal, civil nuclear energy in relation to Sri Lanka and the Land Boundary Agreement with Bangladesh may be recalled here.

Modi has also tried to reach out to the people as well as diverse political and Business Stakeholders in the neighbouring countries. There were crisp comments in Nepali media after his speech in the Constituent Assembly, that what diplomats could not do for last thirty years, Modi delivered in thirty minutes, in terms of bridging the sense of alienation and winning the confidence of the Nepalese. He has successfully created an impression in the neighbouring countries through his visits and speeches that now there is a different India under a different leadership, which is acutely sensitive, respectful and cooperative towards the aspirations and expectations of the neighbouring countries. The Commerce Ministry of India, for instance, has drawn up plans for five years to link up trade issues with manufacturing by suggesting that India will invest in the neighbouring countries and buy products that these countries will manufacture from Indian investments to help them reduce their trade deficit and create jobs in the host countries. Soft lines of credit extended by India earlier have been reconfirmed and upgraded with focus on developing connectivity, energy and tourism. There is a clear emphasis on the developmental.

In Nepal, he did not hesitate to meet Maoists, or anybody who did not necessarily belong to the ruling parties. In Sri Lanka, he met the former President Rajapaksa as well as Chandrika Kumaratunga to convey that

New Delhi is now dealing with the country and not with any specific group of leaders or only those who are in power. As in a chessboard political approach evident during previous regimes, Modi is not looking for his pawns or bishops in the country concerned. His message is that he is interested in a particular country as a whole; its aspirations and its sensitivities. Accordingly, he seems to be redefining India's approach to the neighbouring countries. In the process, Modi is also nudging the processes of democratic transition that have experienced difficulties and hurdles in the neighbouring countries. In Nepal, he went and said, 'consensus should be basis of constitution making'. His Foreign Secretary, S. Jaishankar, reiterated this during his follow-up visit to Nepal. In Sri Lanka, he said, you must build an inclusive society which means that the majority Sinhalese must show accommodation towards the minority Tamils. The cancellation of his visit to Maldives at the last minute was a message of disapproval to the Government in power there on the way the former President Nasheed was being treated.

Modi has also tried to broaden the canvas of India's neighborhood. Jayant has talked about Look East and Act East. Modi has started looking South and South-West as well. His recent visits to Seychelles and Mauritius along with Sri Lanka, was a move in securing the Indian Ocean front. He was also scheduled to visit Maldives but, as stated earlier, internal political turbulence there forced him to postpone his visit. Modi has also brought in the use of soft power, emphasis on cultural and civilisational identities with the neighbours as an important aspect of mutual engagements.

In his efforts for regional cooperation, there is greater thrust on sub-regional cooperation under the assumption that Pakistan may still be obstructing regional integration and India's lead in carrying together the neighbouring countries through SAARC. This was evident during the Kathmandu SAARC Summit in November 2014. Recall his words at that Summit when he said that we will pursue regional bonding within SAARC, if possible and without SAARC, if necessary. This approach though runs the risk of weakening the regional framework, but what alternative there is if Pakistan is not willing to come on board, as was evident at Kathmandu on the question of the proposed Agreement on road, rail and energy connectivity. I think, the Prime Minister has encouraged various Indian Ministries to start working on the eastern sub-regional grouping, where Nepal, Bhutan, Bangladesh and India, can work together and possibly bring Myanmar along. India can also now work closely with Sri Lanka, Maldives, Mauritius and Seychelles to develop a southern sub-regional network. The problem area, in this respect, is Pakistan, which in relation to Afghanistan and India, invokes more security and conflict issues than those of sub-regional cooperation. The idea of emphasis on the eastern sub-region will also hopefully give a message to Pakistan that India's regional approach will not be held hostage to Pakistan's India fixation. This will harm SAARC framework, but what else can be done?

It may be noted here that this is not a new dimension of Modi's approach. India had much earlier, during the late 1990s, created BIMSTEC (Bay of Bengal Initiative for Multi-Sectoral Technological and Economic Cooperation) as if was difficult to get Pakistan to join in promoting SAARC and carrying its programmes forward. BIMSTEC has not been a great success yet. The emphasis on sub-regionalism may not really break SAARC, because the concept is endorsed within the SAARC Charter and consensus. If this can help reorient SAARC and streamline it, even by persuading and pressurising Pakistan, so much the better.

As things stand, Modi's approach towards Pakistan, however, is not helping India resolve its Pakistan dilemma. His Pakistan policy has so far been a flip-flop. There was a flicker of hope when the Modi Government decided to discontinue the India-Pakistan comprehensive dialogue if Pakistan continues to host the *Hurriyat* leaders and consult them on Indo-Pak relations. This position meant a significant message to Pakistan that business was not as usual under the new government, if Kashmiri separatists were being patronised by Pakistan. This position has however, not been sustained by the Modi Government. Hurriyat leaders continue to be hosted by the Pakistan High Commission in New Delhi, and the Modi Government decided to send its Foreign Secretary to Pakistan under the pretext of the so-called SAARC yatra to presumably explore the prospects of restarting talks. This could have been under external pressures, but the hopes aroused of a firm and rational approach to Pakistan were dashed. Later on he met Prime Minister Nawaz Sharif at Ufa in Russia and resumed the process of dialogue culminating in Prime Minister Modi's sudden visit to Lahore on December 25, 2015. Even after the terrorist attack on Pathankot Airbase in early January 2016, the Modi Government has not come up with a firm policy towards Pakistan.

Hence, we are all now under utter confusion as to what is the Modi

Government's and the BJP's Pakistan Policy? What kind of engagement do we want? What kind of pressure we can generate on Pakistan? There is also confusion on the Modi Government's approach towards the Kashmir question. What is our policy towards Pakistan Occupied Kashmir? Is Modi willing to settle along the Line Of Control (LOC) which basically has been India's policy since Nehru and was clearly reflected during the previous UPA government? The former Prime Minister Manmohan Singh publicly claimed that within this framework, he had almost worked out a resolution of the Kashmir issue. In the face of formation of a coalition government with the Peoples' Democratic Party (PDP) in Jammu & Kashmir, it is legitimate to raise the question as to what is the Union government's Kashmir policy.

Ambassador Prasad has dealt with China a great deal. I agree with him and do not want to repeat the points made by him. In Modi's China policy, which falls in a category by itself as a part of India's neighbourhood policy, I was struck by his Press Statement in New Delhi, during the Chinese President Xi's visit. In the presence of President Xi, he made it very clear that while India would want to deepen economic engagement with China, the efforts in this respect will not go very far if China does not address India's strategic and security sensitivities, like the question of border dispute. India has also put forth its concerns regarding continued Chinese military and political support for Pakistan, ignoring its role in encouraging terrorism in the neighbouring countries. China is also worried about Islamic extremism in Pakistan and its spill-over into China's sensitive Xinjiang region. China has almost turned a deaf ear to these Indian concerns. One does not know what options India has in dealing with the Chinese challenge. May be I should revert to this issue briefly later.

Now let me finally come to the challenges that India under Modi faces in its neighbourhood policy. I think the neighborhood policy will face challenges in four areas. One is of internal cohesion, the second is of persisting political and social turbulence within some of our neighbours, the third would be of a spill-over of the 'Western Disturbance', if I may say so, and the fourth is of the pressures generated by the Eastern resurgence i.e. China's rise and assertion. Let me take them up one by one.

Challenges Ahead

With regard to internal cohesion, there are two aspects to be taken note of. One is concerning the administrative and political coordination and bureaucracy's strategic perspective on critical foreign policy issues. Modi's style of functioning is such that he deals with the Secretaries and bureaucrats directly, often bypassing their respective Ministers. His intention may be to get decisions delivered quickly. Indian policy on the whole suffers seriously from what may be called "delivery deficit". However, getting direct results through the concentration of power in the PMO may be easier said than done. There are layers and layers of decision-making that the Prime Minister and his own office cannot reach and penetrate smoothly. This is being gradually realised.

Then there is a question of political coordination at the level of states in a federal polity like India's. New Delhi's neighbourhood policy is most directly affected by the federal pressures as many of India's states share borders with neighbouring countries and have interests and stakes in the issues involved. We all know that India's approach towards Sri Lanka, where the Tamil Nadu factor continues to impinge on the policy, or towards Bangladesh, which has been affected by the position taken by West Bengal—recall the fiasco on the Land Boundary and Teesta water sharing Agreements during Manmohan Singh's visit to Bangladesh in 2013. Such examples can be multiplied regarding the role of Bihar, UP and Uttarakhand in relation to Nepal, Kashmir and Punjab in relation to Pakistan, West Bengal and North-East in relation to Bhutan and Myanmar, and so on. Modi is acutely aware of the federal imperative on India's neighbourhood policy and trying his best to take the concerned states on board. His efforts to cultivate the state leaders like Mamata Bannerjee in West Bengal, Jayalalitha in Tamil Nadu and Mehbooba Mufti and her late father Mufti Mohd. Sayyed in Jammu & Kashmir may be recalled here. There are persisting underlying tensions in this respect and it remains to be seen as to what extent Modi will succeed.

There is yet another aspect of internal coordination in the conduct of the neighbourhood policy that I wish to submit before you. This may be a debatable issue politically but must be scrutinised in academic gatherings like this. In pursuance of his soft power and civilisational approach in his overall foreign policy and especially in the neighbourhood policy, Modi has been emphasising Hinduism and Buddhism, but he has not uttered a word on Islam. I understand that Buddhism and Hinduism, also Sikhism, which he has mentioned in his foreign visits, are the original Indian religions, but Islam is not. But Islam is very much a part of India's composite culture that we all take pride in. Modi, during his visits to the neighbouring and other foreign countries, has visited temples and talked about Buddhist Shrines and places of pilgrims, but has not referred to mosques or Islamic shrines. Has this been an inadvertent slip or a conscious omission? However, his temple visits, like those to the *Pashupatinath* in Nepal, the Hindu Tamil Temple in Sri Lanka, to the Sikh Temple in Canada, send a strong political message not only to his home constituencies but also to the people in the host countries. But the message sent to India's Islamic/Muslim-majority neighbours like Pakistan, Bangladesh, Maldives and Afghanistan becomes negative, particularly to the extremist and radicalised sections of the populations in these countries. This is impinging on the neighbourhood policy in the long run. To add to this, are the voices raised by the radical Hindu sections within India, from the ruling party, which are adding to the fire of Islamic radicals of South Asia. Modi has been either unwilling or incapable of controlling these extremist religious voices of his own party leading to the complications in his otherwise acceptable image in the neighbourhood.

The second area of challenge to Modi's neighbourhood policy comes from political polarisation and turbulence within the neighbouring countries. One must keep it in mind here that India's neighbours already have a big problem vis-à-vis India arising out of huge power imbalance and acute identity convergence. As a result, the neighbourhood politicians and leaders face a dilemma in identifying with India. For them, India is an identity as well as a political problem. Accordingly, there is lack of any national consensus in the neighbouring countries as to how close and in what manner they can and should identify with India without spoiling their political prospects. How close a hug they can politically afford or deepen the degree of alienation from India will profit them politically within their own respective countries remains an unsettled question. This is being further complicated by political rivalries and ideological polarisation which reinforce India as a divisive factor in their mutual dealings. In almost every political division in the neighbouring country, India is a controversial factor. Whether it is in Bangladesh between BNP and Awami League, whether it is in Maldives between Nasheed and his contenders, whether in Nepal between the Maoist and others political parties, India is a dividing factor. How can Indian policy and diplomacy navigate through these divisions is not an easy task. Mr Modi since he has to run the show for another four to five years, has to see how to take India out of these controversies both at the identity level and also on the level of political polarisation.

The other two challenges are external. One, we have been talking about the 'western disturbance' to explain unseasonal rains that destroyed a good deal of crops and fruit output. This is climatic. I am talking of political western disturbance. This is about violence, instability and turbulence in Pakistan, Afghanistan and also the spill-over of Arab spring and rise of the Islamic State. These western political clouds are unpredictable and worrisome. We do not know how will Pakistan settle down into a stable, democratic and non-extremist polity. How will Afghanistan be able to sustain its constitutional democratic structure and evolve into a peaceful, moderate Islamic society? How will Afghanistan and Pakistan work out their bilateral relations? How is West Asia shaping up, particularly its sectarian Shia-Sunni conflict and the power rivalry between Iran and Saudi Arabia? Both these contenders of power and influence in the region have long-term impact on India's energy and remittance futures. India's role in this region is marginal but we will be seriously affected by the developments here. There are reports that South Asia, including some parts of India, are becoming sources of supply even for the IS warriors. The Modi Government does not seem to be paying sufficient attention to this region. After President Ghani's coming to power, India stands marginalised politically as far as Pakistan and Afghanistan are concerned. The problems lies deeply in Pakistan and Afghanistan internally as also between them, but the outcome will affect us and India's neighbourhood policy.

The fourth and the last external challenge is the pressure of the Eastern resurgence; the rise and assertion of China. Ambassador Prasad has talked at length about China already. What I wish to add briefly is that India cannot wish China away in South Asia. China has developed strong economic and strategic stakes to reinforce and expand its presence in South Asia. In order to keep its turbulent Tibetan and Xinjiang regions stable and developing, it needs cooperation and understanding from the South Asian countries. In order to resolve its Malacca dilemma, of protecting energy trade through the Malacca Strait and Indian Ocean, China needs a strong presence in the Bay of Bengal and thus cooperation with the countries like Pakistan, Sri Lanka, Maldives, Myanmar, Bangladesh, etc. These countries can also help China divert its strategic trade through land routes as is being envisaged through the Gwadar port and the proposed $40bn China-Pakistan economic corridor. Then South Asia, a region of 1.6bn people, growing at the rate of 5–65 annually if not more, constitutes a huge economic market which China, or any other growing economy cannot ignore. Both the market potential and trade security imperatives have prompted China to come up with the projects like Maritime Silk Road and belt. Lastly, if China has to counter the new US strategy of rebalance aimed to contain it in the Asia-Pacific region, then it has to befriend, among others, South and South-East Asian countries. We will therefore see more and more of the Chinese push towards South Asia in the coming months and years. Modi and his successors may have to evolve a credible strategy to cope with China in South Asia. Modi's strategists are proposing various options ranging from revisiting the Tibet policy to piggy-backing the US in dealing with China. This however is a long term, and one of the formidable challenges for India.

When it comes to India-China relations, there are clearly two narratives: one is a cooperative, co-existence narrative and the other is a conflict narrative. The cooperative narrative goes back to the seventeenth and eighteenth centuries when since the First Century AD, China and India had both grown without conflict or rivalry with each other. Nehru's approach of peaceful coexistence, and Dr Manmohan Singh's dictum of the world having enough space for both China and India to grow simultaneously, were rooted into this cooperative narrative. The US strategy of "rebalance" in the Asia-Pacific region, in the view of many analysts seeks a negation of this narrative as it tries to balance one emerging Asian power against the other(s). Both India and China have to seriously ponder over the imperatives of the US policy for what is being promised as the Asian Century. They have to think seriously if they have to build the Asian Century or allow the US balance under the US leadership to grow. It is more for China to think about it because if wants the Asian Century to be created, then China has to resolve its disputes and problems with the other Asian neighbours, including India. The conflict narrative that cropped up between India and China since the late fifties and particularly following China's military aggression against India in 1962 is not the answer to the promise of the Asian Century. For the cooperative narrative to unfold and get reinforced, China has to address India's sensitivities on borders, in relation to Pakistan and in relation to other South Asian neighbours. India on its part may have to reassure China that it will not play the game of "rebalancing" strategy. India may also respond positively to Chinese proposals of economic reconstruction in Asia and South Asia, including to the Maritime Silk Road. Soon after its independence, India had taken a positive lead in working for Asian solidarity and development. Why it is that India has been lagging behind China in its Asian initiatives?

For instance, with regard to the Chinese proposal of Maritime Silk Road, rather than shying away from a concrete response, India may offer China access to Indian Ocean to through Calcutta-Sikkim Corridor, provided China is willing to invest in upgrading the Kolkata port, and allowing access to the Chumbi Valley. This can be offered, provided China assures two things to India. One, it will expedite drawing the Line of Actual Control and secondly it will exit from the POK. This is how India can take initiatives in engaging China towards building a mutual inter-dependence. Another bold initiative on India's part towards China could be to sound out the Chinese on the return of the Dalai Lama and his Dharamsala government, provided, and this is an important precondition, China accepts an internationally monitored guarantee for the human and cultural rights to the all Tibetans. The point that I wish to underline is that there is considerable scope for Modi's government to think out of box and take bold initiatives in engaging China both economically and strategically, bilaterally as also within the regional South Asian context.

3

India's Diplomatic Leap in South Asia

Anoop Kumar Gupta

Introduction

India's South Asia policy has witnessed drastic changes in the post-cold war period with elements of continuity.[1] In order to play any decisive role at the global level, it is very important for a rising and emerging power like India to correct and consolidate its relations with its immediate neighbours and transform the region into an engine for growth and development for the well-being of the people of the subcontinent. An ambitious three stage road map for visualising new South Asia, i.e. a South Asia Free Trade Area, followed by a Custom Union and a broader Economic Union by the year 2020 is still away from realisation.[2]

Domestic political compulsion, regional dynamics and global configuration have played important roles in determining, shaping and making India's regional policy. Historically speaking, implementation of India's South Asian policy witnessed three patterns overlapping with each other in some way or another. While formulating its regional policy, India looked towards the region from three prisms that are international, regional and domestic. Looking from the Internationalist prism, India watched the region from global structural realities. A kaleidoscopic view of the region from the domestic prism compelled India to give priorities to its domestic political compulsion over the strategic requirement of the regional architecture. A peep in to the region from the regional prism reflected the accommodative or assertive posture as conceived by a strategic cultural paradigm that prevailed over the then leadership. The NDA II regime under the leadership of PM Narendra Modi has looked towards its immediate neighbourhood from the regional prism while keeping into account the domestic, trans-regional and global realities. The Modi regime has displayed an accommodative and cooperative approach towards the neighbourhood in order to write the script of a shared growth story while keeping a vigilant eye on India's national interests.

The foreign policy initiatives of the National Democratic Alliance or NDA II under PM Narendra Modi's dispensation witnessed a splendid balance between India's regional engagements and global diplomatic activism. India's hectic diplomatic engagement under the NDA II regime with global powers and middle powers did not ignored its focus on immediate neighbourhood since the beginning as was witnessed with the oath ceremony in which the heads of all seven South Asian neighbours and Mauritius were invited. It seems that India's regional policy is entering a new era since the emergence of PM Narendra Modi-led full majority NDA II regime at the centre.

General Policy Perspective

In order to give a new and speedy dimension to India's growth story, PM Modi-led NDA II regime has displayed diplomatic activism at regional and global levels since the beginning. This reflects the policy perspective and vision of India's foreign engagement under his dispensation. While core values like self-reliance, strategic autonomy, national security, economic development remain unchanged, diplomatic behaviour and foreign policy orientation witnessed remarkable changes under Modi's dispensation. One can observe a certain pattern of diplomatic behaviour since the emergence of PM Narendra Modi-led full majority BJP government at the centre.

The NDA II regime under PM Modi has put forth the focus on 'India first' and its national interests emphatically not only in the economic field but also on security issues and new red lines have been drawn in this regard. These red lines have been demonstrated in India's engagement with Pakistan, China, WTO, terrorism and climate change. Now the extra-emphasis is on capability building in a neo-structural paradigm in order to envisage a civilisational global role for India. The innovative concept of 'Make in India', 'Digital India', and 'Skill India' have been started for the same. Capability building is conceived in developing India's hard power that included not only developing military power and capability but also economic and technological development. The Modi regime is significantly utilising the tools of diplomacy to help reinvigorate India's economy through pitching for foreign direct investment and export promotion.

The change in the conduct of diplomacy is clearly visible in terms of style and emphasis under the NDA II regime. It has been termed as 'fast track diplomacy' which is 'pro-active, strong and sensitive'. It seems that foreign policy behaviour under PM Modi is moving beyond ideology and non-alignment. It is focused on teleological, inclusive energetic foreign relations and dynamic diversification scheme based on multi-alignment. It also seems to have moved beyond 'Nehruvian idealism' and 'neo-liberal orthodoxy'. Modi regime is emphatically integrating India's cultural, spiritual and philosophical legacy to foreign policy and giving a new dimension to India's soft power. Para-Diplomacy is on an up-swing and Indian federal units and cities are supposed to play a bigger role in economic diplomacy in terms of town twinning agreement and sister state agreement.

South Asian Policy

India's engagement with South Asian neighbours witnessed a diplomatic dynamism and activism to foster economic growth and enhance the security environment. Being free from political compulsions of a coalition government, the NDA II regime has adopted multi-layered regional policy orientation which included regional integration and sub-regional cooperation based on commonly shared destiny on neo-functional argument, bilateral and intra-regional trade and investment promotion in neo-liberal economic perspective, accommodative approach to the rational and just demands of its neighbours in liberal-democratic ethos, while not ignoring the questions of national security challenges involving neo-realist paradigm.

Neighbourhood First Policy

One of the major policy initiatives of PM Modi's foreign policy is 'neighbourhood first' which aimed at concentrating on immediate neighbours and give emphasis on improving relations with these states in the South Asian region. Concentrating on the immediate neighbourhood, PM Modi initiated the 'neighbourhood first' policy in order to correct and improve bilateral relations. This policy has generated good will in the regional environment. Zero-problem neighbourhood with economic interdependence is the primary goal of this policy initiative. The objective of the 'neighbourhood first' policy initiatives in South Asia is to promote regional, sub-regional and bilateral connectivity and economic cooperation, limit the influence of extra-territorial rival powers and minimise and control radical and extremist forces. This is a prerequisite for India to play any decisive role beyond this region.

Immediately after the victory of the NDA in the general elections in May 2014, an invitation was extended to SAARC leaders to attend the swearing-in of the new Cabinet. This witnessed the focus and priority of NDA II on the immediate neighbourhood and was described as a 'master stroke' in regional diplomacy. Within one year of his regime PM Modi visited Bhutan, Nepal, Sri Lanka and Bangladesh in order to cement the bilateral ties. The External Affairs Minister, Foreign Secretary and National Security Advisor gave due place to South Asian states in order to visualise NDA II regime's 'the region first policy'.

Focus on Regional Integration

Neo-functionalism finds a way in PM Modi's South Asia policy in order to promote and enhance regional integration in the region. Strengthening regional integration and bilateral economic relations emerged as a primary goal. Intra-regional trade is very low at present.

Ahead of his Nepal visit to attend the SAARC summit, PM Modi said that development of close relations with neighbours was a key priority for his government.[3] He also stated that India has always emphasised on the importance of greater regional integration at all levels for the socio-economic development of the South Asian region. NDA II has undertaken several initiatives in this regard on bilateral, sub-regional and regional basis.

Emphasising the need for better connectivity in the region PM Modi has concluded that "Our relations become stronger when we connect the lives of the ordinary citizens of our countries. That is why connectivity and services by rail and road are so important. We should also connect ourselves more by air".[4] He further stressed that "for India, our vision for the region rests on five pillars – trade, investment, assistance, cooperation in every area, contacts between our people – and, all through seamless connectivity".

For increasing the connectivity in the region, the Modi regime has initiated signing of SAARC (South Asia Association for Regional Co-operation) connectivity agreements including Motor Vehicle pacts during the 18th SAARC summit in Nepal in November 2014. Though SAARC leaders agreed upon energy cooperation, they could not agree on connectivity issues. Pakistan has blocked two rail and road connectivity initiatives on the pretext of completing its 'internal process'.[5] India wanted to promote regional connectivity in the region as was witnessed at the SAARC summit. However, the SAARC summit ended with the Kathmandu Declaration that called for deeper regional cooperation in core areas of trade, investment, finance, energy, infrastructure and connectivity.[6] In a neo-structural analysis, SAARC represent relatively a weak regional organisation which has a long way to go ahead in order to realise the establishment of the South Asia Union. In order to promote the spirit of regional cooperation, PM Modi proposed the establishment of SAARC Bank and SAARC satellite for regional development.

Ahead of displaying its commitments for regional integration, India is also moving with its other neighbours at bilateral and sub-regional levels for enhancing connectivity and cooperation in other fields. For this purpose India has initiated bilateral connectivity, power and other agreements with countries within SAARC. The Motor Vehicle Agreement with Nepal was signed in this regard. This envisages the regular bus services between the two countries. India and Bangladesh started bus services between the two countries. In order to raise the connectivity at sub-regional level, India, Bangladesh, Bhutan and Nepal have agreed for an easy movement of goods through road transport. India has also moved ahead with a neo-liberal argument and ethos in order to enhance trade and investment relations. PM Modi has also emphasised the trilateral cooperation among India, Sri Lanka and Maldives in the Indian Ocean Region which is meticulously extended up to Mauritius and Seychelles.

Visualisation of Human Security

Social indicators in terms of health, wealth and education of the major portion of the population in the region involve the question of human security. During the SAARC summit in Nepal, PM Modi emphasised that "big and small we face the same challenges – a long climb to the summit of development". He also indicated that collective efforts are needed in the case of South Asia to deal with common challenges. He wanted to 'make difference to the lives of our people' in the region and stated that the 'future I dream for India is the future I wish for our entire region'. PM Modi gave a call to 'work to change cynicism into optimism' and 'turn South Asia of flowering hope into a rich field of peace and prosperity'. India also extended its humanitarian relief work to its small neighbours in the time of crisis. India was quick to help Maldives during the wake of drinking water crisis in the country. India sent its heavy lift transporter like C 17 Globe Master III and Il-76 with water bottles to Maldives to rescue it from the water crisis. The Indian Navy also sent its ships like INS Sukanya and INS Deepak which have on board desalination plants to produce fresh water on the spot. In the same manner, India extended its quick humanitarian help to earthquake-hit Nepal.

Liberal Ethos for Upgradation of Ties

Confidence building for giving a new shape to bilateral relations with its immediate neighbours is the most important goal of NDA II regime. Keeping in the mind the tone and tenor of the Gujral Doctrine of being non-reciprocal towards regional partners, NDA II regime has extended help to its small but strategically important neighbours. In order to strengthen a 'unique and special relationship' with Bhutan, PM Modi chose to visit the small Bhutanese state as his first foreign destination. Apart from cementing business ties including hydropower projects, the issue of insurgency in North-East India and China were also discussed with Bhutan. India has built a trauma centre at Kathamandu's Bir Hospital. One billion line of credit has been announced to Nepal in August 2014. India also decided to help by building a police training academy in Nepal to train over 400 police officers annually.[7] India has gifted Nepal a HAL advanced light helicopter to the Nepali army.

Attempts are being made by the Modi regime to upgrade the nature of bilateral relations with all South Asian neighbours. Sri Lanka and Maldives are important for India's maritime security structure in the Indian Ocean Region. Things seem to be changing positively in the Indo-Sri Lankan relations with the emergence of Maithripala Sirisena in the 2015 presidential election. Sirisena's victory would tilt towards China. In order to cement the bilateral ties India signed a civil nuclear agreement with Sri Lanka. During PM Modi's visit to Sri Lanka in March 2015, India signed four agreements in the areas of visa, customs, youth development and building the Rabindranath Tagore memorial. India reiterated its commitment to help Trincomalee become a petroleum hub and announced a fresh Line of Credit of up to 318 million USD for the railway sector in Sri Lanka.

In an attempt to reduce the major irritants between India and Bangladesh, the Indian Parliament ratified Land Border Agreement with Bangladesh. During PM Modi's visit to Bangladesh both the countries ratified the LBA. India has given two billion Line of Credit to Bangladesh during PM Modi's visit to that country. Both the countries also solved the long due maritime boundary dispute which was hailed by the international community as a role model for resolving the maritime dispute in the South China Sea. In reference to the concern of the Nepalese political community regarding the India-Nepal Treaty of Peace and Friendship of 1950, PM Modi expressed India's readiness to revisit and revise the same. The political elite in Nepal since long have termed the treaty as unequal which has been a source of fomenting anti-India feelings in Nepal.

Cooperative Federalism

In order to give a thrust to its 'neighbourhood first' policy, Modi regime ensured the cooperation of federal units in promoting and cementing ties with immediate neighbours. Regionalisation of the South Asian policy is positively witnessed in Indo-Bangladesh relations. NDA II has tried to win the confidence of the West Bengal Chief Minister in order to felicitate the success of Land Border Agreement and connectivity links between India and Bangladesh. At the same time, the Modi regime has successfully denied the pressure of the regional political parties to have any negative influence on regional policy. It has ignored the demand of the political parties of Tamil Nadu during the oath ceremony for not inviting the Sri Lankan president.

Act East Policy

PM Modi has blended his 'neighbourhood first' policy with 'Act East' policy which seeks to rejuvenate India's ties with its extended neighbourhood in South East Asia and East Asia. He emphasised that 'India's Act East Policy starts with Bangladesh' in a bid to forge a step-ahead extra-regional geo-economic linkage between South Asia and South-East Asia. Through Bangladesh, India wants to connect North-East India with the rest of India for easy, smooth and speedy transit and wishes to reach out further to the South-East Asian nations. Modi also proposed to develop a link between South Asia and Central Asia for the benefit of both the regions during his maiden visit to Central Asia in July 2015.

National Security Concerns

If neo-functionalism, neo-liberalism and liberal ethos are the core assumptions of Modi regime's South Asia policy, it did not relinquish the neo-structuralism or neo-realist argument as far as threat to India's national security is concerned. Apart from pitching for regional integration ethos and sub-regional and bilateral initiatives to promote multilateral cooperation in the region, the Modi regime has displayed an assertive defence posture in dealing with security concerns and challenges including the issues of trans-border terrorism from Pakistan, the increasing level of border incursion in Ladakh by the PLA and maintenance of strategic stability in Afghanistan. An assertive defence strategy could also be seen in a hot pursuit operation against insurgency in north-eastern India.

Maintaining strategic stability and peace in Afghanistan is a priority issue for India as Indian security establishment feared a potential revival of terrorist forces in the country and subcontinent after the withdrawal of US-led NATO troops. India appreciated the move of the new Afghan regime under President Ashraf Ghani to sign a bilateral security agreement with the United States which will pave the way for stationing around 10,000 American troops. External Affairs Minister Sushma Swaraj not only described India as Afghanistan's first strategic partner but also reiterated India's commitment to play a significant role in capacity building of the Afghan National Army. In order to ensure its access to landlocked Afghanistan and beyond to bolster its trade, investment and security link, India has signed an agreement with Iran to develop and modernise Chabahar Port. India has been hesitant in sending troops and exporting military equipments to Afghanistan. India has an arrangement with Afghanistan according to which it would pay for purchase of arms and ammunition from the Russian Federation.

Counter-terrorism is the main thrust of India's regional and global diplomacy. The Modi regime has given emphasis to counter-terrorism efforts at regional and global levels. In a bid to mobilise global support for counter-terror diplomacy, India succeeded in pursuing the US to incorporate the cooperation on the issue of terrorism in a joint statement. Terrorism is proving a stumbling block in the rise of India as it threatens not only the national development but also internal security.

Issue of trans-border terrorism is the main obstacle in the normalisation of relations between India and Pakistan. Pakistan is becoming a difficult neighbour and the NDA II regime's policy is that there could be no meaningful dialogue under the shadow of cross-border terrorism, ceasefire violation, infiltration manoeuvring and the slow progress of Mumbai attack trails. How India should respond to Pakistan belligerences? There are two schools in Indian strategic community regarding Pakistan policy: first school includes the hawks who believe in following the 'punish Pakistan policy'; second school consists of doves who believe in 'engaging Pakistan policy'.

As a part of the comprehensive policy regarding Pakistan, the Modi regime tried to engage the Pak civil authority while keeping India's security concern a top priority. The Modi regime has displayed a duality in its approach towards Pakistan. On the one hand it has expressed the goodwill gesture towards the country and invited Pakistani PM Nawaz Sharif to the oath ceremony of the new regime in order to engage Pakistan and greeted him on the pious occasion of Ramzan and assured the freeing of Pakistani fishermen. On the other hand it displayed hard posturing towards the Mumbai attack trail case and policy of massive retaliation towards cross-border terrorism and ceasefire violations. Thus the Modi regime displayed a mix of using the diplomatic tools for promoting or holding dialogue with its political counterpart as the situations unfold themselves and adhering to massive military retaliation to adventurism at border by the Pakistani military establishment or its non-state actor agents. India demonstrated its red lines regarding trans-border terrorism, ceasefire violations and trial of Mumbai attack mastermind Lakhvi. India cancelled the proposed Foreign Secretary level talks scheduled on August 25, 2014 in Islamabad following Pakistani High Commissioner Abdul Basit's meeting with separatist leaders of Jammu and Kashmir. India also mobilised world opinion against terrorism. India also raised the case of release of Lakhvi at the United Nations under 1267 clause; however, China held the move in the committee, quoting technical issues.

India responded with 'double force' to Pakistani attempts to violate the sanctity of the Line of Control. The Modi regime overcomes the debate regarding the dilemma of India's option of employing military retaliation with Pakistan in the event of border incursion in nuclear South Asia.[8] 'Cold Start' doctrine for limited war fighting strategy, which was unveiled in 2004 in a bid to answer the conundrum posed by this nuclear situation, did not find a way in some or other form on ground as the UPA regime relied on diplomacy rather than massive military retaliation to check border violations.[9] The Mumbai attack in 2008 tended the analyst to conclude that 'India did not have capacity to punish Pakistan'[10] and there are 'fundamental weakness in Indian national security policy.'[11] Conversely, while focussing on the national security question seriously, the Modi regime did not allow Pakistan to continue and undertake low intensity conflict at the border under the shadow of nuclear umbrella. India has moved to adopt limited military action with massive retaliation to deter border incursion by the Pakistani military establishment and also taken care of avoiding the conflict reaching full escalation. Modi regime responded with limited but massive military action against Pakistan in an attempt to nullify Pakistan sub-conventional strategy.

While maintaining the hard-posturing at the border, the Modi regime always extended its goodwill gesture to Pakistan on many occasions in order to keep the door open for diplomacy. In order to realise the shared destiny of South Asia based on neo-functional, neo-liberal and liberal-democratic ethos, the Modi regime tried to reach out to Pakistan with firmness on national security issues. That effort finally resulted in the Ufa spirit. The Ufa meeting between the Prime Ministers of India and Pakistan, during the sidelines of the SCO meeting in Russia, signalled the Modi regime's readiness to engage Pakistan while ensuring its security concerns. India responded positively once Pakistan showed its willingness to condemn terrorism and expedite trials of Mumbai culprits. Pakistan agreed with India to cooperate in condemning and eliminating terrorism and ensuring peace. For that purpose National Security Advisors of both the countries will hold dialogues followed by military level engagement for maintaining peace at the border. PM Modi's diplomatic synergy around the globe and firmness displayed at the border might have compelled the Pakistani political regime to consider India's redlines regarding national security and counter-terrorism. PM Modi's strategy proved successful at least for now in setting the tone and tenor of the agenda during the Ufa dialogue.

The road map that is enshrined in the Ufa joint statement would be tested on the ground. A former diplomat and expert on Pakistan Parthasarathy does recognise the need to maintain "healthy skepticism" until concrete action is taken. "Ultimately this relationship's direction will depend on terrorism and the situation on the borders". "The proof of the pudding is in the eating," he says. "Don't forget we had great agreements in Lahore [during Vajpayee's visit] and then we had Kargil [war of 1999] within three months".[12] The result of Ufa bonhomie will depend on internal structural compulsions of Pakistani politics. Continued ceasefire violation and increased infiltration bid followed by Ufa spirit reflect the mindset of the military establishment of Pakistan and internal contradictions of the Pakistani political structure. These attempts aimed at violating the Ufa spirit. Issues related to voice samples of Lakhvi, its obsession with Kashmir, so-called fabricated shooting down of drones have been raised in Pakistan immediately after the Ufa agreement in order to console its domestic constituency.

Decisive structural independent variables within Pakistani politics like the perception of ISI, Army and religious ultra-orthodox groups towards India need acute transformation for the success of normalisation of bilateral ties and establishment of friendly and cordial relations. Politics of identity in Pakistan is deeply associated with anti-India idioms. That is why, constructivism involving the question of identity and ideational force, rather than rationalist-materialist theories like classical realism, structural-realism, complex interdependence and neo-liberalism explains Pakistani strategic behaviour towards India. If this strategic culture in the Pakistani establishment persists then it is very difficult, if not impossible, to improve India-Pakistan ties. Discussing the prospects of India–Pakistan relations, a prominent expert has concluded that "as long as the Army, directly or indirectly remains the final arbiter of all national decisions-making there will be no normalisation of relations between India and Pakistan".[13] Perceptional change particularly in the Pakistani military establishment is needed for the reflection of change at the ground reality regarding ceasefire violation, cross-border infiltration and cross-border terrorism. The Modi regime needs to take this consideration into account while engaging with Pakistan. Any paradigm shift in bilateral relations requires a new thinking and constructive ideational transformation of the Pakistani military elite's anti-India mindset.

Sensitivities towards the Great Game

Learning lessons from the Great Game of the 19th century in Asia between British India and Imperial Russia, independent India tried hard to keep the extra-regional power away from the Indian subcontinent. However, these attempts met with little success as India could not stop the detrimental meddling of the United States in cold war days and disadvantageous building of 'string of pearls' by China in post-cold war days in this subcontinent. Increasing presence and influence of China in India's neighbourhood caused a serious concern in South Block circles. The Modi regime might have realised that involvement of external powers like China in the region could not be restricted just by protesting and criticising the footholds of outside power in the region. That is why PM Modi has initiated the well thought out and purposeful 'neighbourhood first' policy whose one major aim seems to minimise the prospects of external involvement to such an extent that it is detrimental to its national security. Keeping this factor in mind PM Modi wants to change the gear of subcontinental interaction that would be based on cooperative regionalism and shared destiny. NDA II has displayed it serious commitment to build the high level of confidence in the subcontinent apart from promoting regional integration, removing irritants in bilateral ties and developing friendly relations with immediate neighbours. Apart from pushing for economic regionalism in the subcontinent, NDA II has also focussed rigorously on internal balancing in terms of capacity building and overall development of comprehensive national power. Demonstrating the wisdom of ancient Indian realist thinker Chanakya's *Mandala* theory formulation, India under PM Modi activated diplomatic effort in the extended neighbourhood in omni-direction. Implementing the rule of external balancing in the east of India the Modi regime witnessed no inhibition to expand cooperation with Japan, Vietnam and Philippines along with the United States in the Indo-Pacific region. India also activated ocean diplomacy in the south, reached out to Central Asian states in the north and in developing close relations with Israel and Arab and Gulf states on the western flank.

Conclusion

As was witnessed in the past, bilateral relations amung South Asian nations have influenced the concrete shaping of cooperative regionalism on neo-functional basis. Despite various themes of regional cooperation, India's bilateral tension with its neighbour in some way or another could not translate cooperative regional ethos into external reality. That is why the Modi regime has focussed on reducing and eliminating the issue of irritants with its neighbours. Without this the South Asian vision could not be materialised.

Foreign policy under Modi's dispensation has displayed a mix of inclusive cultural nationalism, neo-structuralism, neo-liberalism and neo-realism in his South Asia policy. A fine blending of geo-economics and geopolitics with nationalist fervour has been demonstrated in India's diplomatic engagement in this regard.

Thus grand strategic preferences at operational level under the dispensation of PM Modi have reflected the emergence of new strategic thinking in the discourse of India's strategic culture. PM Modi envisaged an innovative and energetic element in the evolution of India's strategic behaviour and strategic preferences. The Modi regime did not adhere to any particular prism of strategic paradigm that is being reflected in the form of Nehruvianism, neo-liberalism and hyper-realism in the strategic community regarding thought-provoking discourse on India's strategic culture. India's strategic culture under PM Modi has displayed a splendid and impressive balance between the ideal-politic paradigm and real-politic paradigm and accordingly demonstrated a set of strategic preferences at operational level in order to safeguard and protect the core values in the domestic, regional and global environment. This reminds us of the strategic culture of the ancient Indic world expressed in classical texts like the *Ramayana*, *Mahabharata*, *Gita* and *Arthashastra* which had displayed the unique and exceptional grand balance between realism and idealism. Based on such unique assumptions and prescriptions, rising India's grand strategy under PM Modi has focused on building a strong, vibrant and self-reliant India in order to transform the Asian century into India's favour and achieve a rightful place for the nation in the global world order so that India could play a leading role.

REFERENCES

1. Chakrabarti, Shantanu, 'India's regional policy making in post Cold War setting', *Societal Studies*, Lithuvania: Mykalos Romeris University, 2012, Vol. 4(2), pp. 407-425; see also Ranjan, Amit (2014) "India's South Asia policy: time to reinvigorate", *ICWA Brief*, 2014 December 24, URL: http://icwa.in/pdfs/PB/2014/IndiasouthasiaPB122014.pdf.
2. Prasad, Jayant (2014), "Rebuilding a regional architecture", *The Hindu*, 24

November, 2014, URL: http://www.thehindu.com/opinion/lead/rebuilding-a-regional-architecture/article6627435.ece

3 "Close ties with neighbours top priority: Prime Minister Narendra Modi", *Economic Times*, 25 November 2014, URL: http://economictimes.indiatimes.com/news/politics-and-nation/close-ties-with-neighbours-top-priority-prime-minister-narendra-modi/articleshow/45267246.cms

4 "Disappointment at Saarc as Pakistan blocks 3 key connectivity agreements", *Times of India*, 26 November 2014, URL: http://timesofindia.indiatimes. com/world/south-asia/Disappointment-at-Saarc-as-Pakistan-blocks-3-key-connectivity-agreements/articleshow/45282809.cms

5. Ibid.

6. "Saarc summit: Energy pact sealed, road and rail pacts on anvil (Roundup)", *Business Standard*, November 27, 2014, URL: http://www.business-standard.com/article/news-ians/saarc-summit-energy-pact-sealed-road-and-rail-pacts-on-anvil-roundup-114112701332_1.html

7. "PM Narendra Modi signs 10 agreements with Nepal, inaugurates bus service", *Times of India*, 26 November 2014, URL: http://timesofindia.indiatimes.com/india/PM-Narendra-Modi-signs-10-agreements-with-Nepal-inaugurates-bus-service/articleshow/45278008.cms

8. For the discussion of impact of nuclear weapon on strategic stability in South Asia and India's option, see Sumit Ganguly, 'Nuclear Stability in South Asia', Bajpai, Kanti and Harsh V. Pant (eds. 2013), "India's National Security", New Delhi: Oxford University Press, pp. 333-359. Kapur, S. Paul (2013), "Ten Years of Instability in South Asia" in Bajpai and Harsh V. Pant (eds.), *India's National Security*, New Delhi: Oxford University Press, pp. 360-385.

9. For the analysis of India's Cold Start doctrine, see Ladwing III, Walter C (2013), "A Cold Start for Hot Wars? The Indian Army's New Limited War Doctrine" in Kanti Bajpai and Harsh V. Pant (eds.), *India's National Security*, New Delhi: Oxford University Press, pp. 386-424.

10. Gupta, Shekhar (2013), "No First Use Options", cited in Kanti Bajpai and Harsh V. Pant (eds.), 'Introduction', of *India's National Security*, New Delhi: Oxford University Press, p. 1.

11. Bajpai, Kanti and Harsh V. Pant (2013), "Introduction", in Kanti Bajpai and Harsh V. Pant (eds.), *India's National Security*, New Delhi: Oxford University Press, p. 1.

12. "India's Narendra Modi to visit Pakistan in 2016 as regional foes continue dialogue", *Time*, 10 July 2015, URL: http://time.com/3952559/narendra-modi-pakistan-visit-nawaz-sharif-ufa-russia-sco-summit-talks/

13. Bahadur, Kalim (2005), "India-Pakistan Relations" in N.S. Sisodia and C. Uday Bhaskar (eds.), *Emerging India: Security and Foreign Policy Perspective*, New Delhi: IDSA, p. 271.

4

Dealing with Pakistan: From a Liberal to a Realist Perspective

Nalini Kant Jha and K.R. Sreelekha

Having shared a common history, culture, polity and economy until 1947, India and Pakistan were destined to be separated by the Partition Plan of the subcontinent under the British imperialism. The partition has created a situation where India has to share its north, north-western and eastern border territories with states that are hostile towards India. This factor has compelled India to adopt an approach called 'continentalism'[1] while formulating its foreign policy priorities. A change in power centre in New Delhi on May 2014 resulted in the reprioritization of foreign policy objectives and approaches in India's foreign policy realm. Thereafter, the region witnessed a detrimental competition between both the states. The partition of the Indian subcontinent in 1947 created two successor states namely, India and Pakistan. The new government that had taken charge under the leadership of Prime Minister Narendra Modi, signalled a change in the conventional way of engagement with Pakistan. There were speculations over the course the new government's foreign policy would take towards Pakistan due to the ruling party's ideological features, known for its hard-line national security perceptions. Such speculations were washed away when Prime Minister Narendra Modi invited all the 'heads of governments' of South Asian states to attend the new government's 'oath of office ceremony'.

India-Pak Relations: South Asian Context

India's foreign policy's course towards Pakistan has greatly been influenced by historical factors. The modern history of the South Asian region has witnessed the partition, bifurcation and cessation of states which were once a part of British India. But it is the partition of the Indian subcontinent in 1947 that banged the region so badly. The partition had created a situation where the new state that was born out of India turned inimical towards India. Sharing lengthy borders with united Pakistan in the western and eastern side and with China on the northern side has forced India to embrace a posture based on territorial defence and the practice still continues as a convention. As in the case of Pakistan, geographically, 'the United Pakistan' was not 'united' in the actual sense of the fact that the two wings of Pakistan – West Pakistan and East Pakistan – were separated by a 1000-mile Indian territory lying in between. This has caused the increase in xenophobia in Pakistan and has raised security concerns. A fragile political system, inability of civilian political leadership to meet the crisis situations and lack of democratic institutions paved way for emergence of 'the Army' – the single most organized institution in Pakistan – to step into the shoe of 'a political force' to deal with the crisis. Immediately after partition, when India was busy building a 'welfare state' and democratic representative institutions, Pakistan had not even completed the 'nation building' process but had been eager to strengthen its military capacity to rectify the imbalance with India. This contradiction of attitudes and values is still reflected in the Indo-Pak dialogue and bilateral process; while India symbolize a representative democracy, Pakistan represents a fragile political institutional set up indirectly controlled by the military establishment. Hence, the priorities are different for a representative democracy and state dominated by military establishment. Whereas India tends to work towards long term strategic and economic unity, Pakistan lacks this regional vision, and time and again Pakistan's identity is often defined by its opposition to and rejection of India.[2] India's ambition to bring better unity and prosperity in South Asia has been undermined by Pakistan's unproductive and uncooperative policies. Thus India-Pakistan bilateralism represents a lingering dialogue between long term vision versus short term strategy. For India, a new government took charge under the leadership of Narendra Modi in May 2014. There were speculations over the course the new government's foreign policy would take towards Pakistan due to the ideological features of the ruling party, known for its hard-line national security perceptions. Such speculations faded away when Prime Minister Narendra Modi invited all the South Asian heads of state on the inaugural day of his government and declared his "neighbourhood first" policy immediately thereafter.

An improved relationship between India and Pakistan is a necessary condition to ensure peace and security in the region. Hence, as one of the largest democracies in the world, India has the responsibility to bring Pakistan into the dialogue process and work out a peaceful settlement of contentious issues.

New Initiatives: Out of the Box Approach

Prime Minister Modi was quick to pronounce his 'neighbourhood first policy' immediately after his accession to power. The meeting of the premiers of both India and Pakistan immediately after the swearing-in ceremony generated enthusiasm and bonhomie in the bilateral process. Since the inception of the Modi government, the Prime Minister has played an important role in articulating the foreign policy priorities of India. There has been significant revival in India's foreign policy course towards Pakistan. Though Prime Minister Modi embraced a proactive foreign policy initiative towards Pakistan, the course was no different from the age-old practice of 'engagement-disengagement-revival of engagement'. To a great extent, Modi succeeded in articulating his trademark 'personal diplomacy' to bring Pakistan into the dialogue process. The bonhomie developed immediately after the swearing-in of the Indian Prime Minister Narendra Modi, unfolded gradually into a trade talk initiative between India and Pakistan[3] and their commitment to initiate Foreign Secretary level talks between both states.[4] But, when the decisions were on the take-off stage, India witnessed violations of ceasefire and a beginning of border skirmishes. From mid-July 2014, there were intense ceasefire violations that lasted until the end of August 30, 2014. By the time, the Government of India had called off the bilateral talks. So, the intention behind propagations of such violence across the border was clear, that they were against a peaceful resolution of the issue. This is the ground reality in Pakistan—no civilian government is free from the military establishment's design on foreign and defence policy.

The positive signal from the civilian leadership towards the Ufa engagement proves the civilian government's attentiveness to go ahead with democratic bilateral engagements, but the Pakistan army was steadfast in appointing a retired army general Nasser Khan Januja as the country's new National Security Advisor, to capturing the NSA,[5] signalling the powerful army's increasing grip on the security affairs of the country and its dealings with India. This sort of conduct from the Pakistan army has made it difficult to imagine Januja being at Prime Minister Nawaz Sharif's side and an Ufa-type declaration being approved by the Pakistan's military establishment.

After several months of disengagement, leaders of both the states exchanged a brief conversation on the sidelines of Climate Change Conference in Paris on December 1, 2015.[6] This meeting was followed by India's External Affairs Minister's participation in the 'Heart of Asia' conference held in Islamabad in December 2015. In her speech she focused on increased connectivity and regional trade and openness with Afghanistan, and extended India's hand towards Pakistan in this regard.[7] An unexpected episode happened in the diplomatic history of Indo-Pak relations, when the Indian Prime Minister made a quick stopover in Lahore to wish his Pakistani counterpart Nawaz Sharif on the occasion of the latter's birthday on December 25, 2015. It is apparent that the gestures expressed by both leaders disseminate the message that they are really committed towards resolving Indo-Pak issues. The Pakistan army and the ISI reacted reprehensibly towards Pak civilian government's active engagement with India. Consequently, India witnessed two terrorist attacks on its sovereign territory: the first terrorist attack was on January 2, 2016 in Pathankot in the Indian state of Punjab and the second terrorist attack took place on January 3, 2016 against the Indian Consulate located in Mazar-i-Sharif in Afghanistan. These two attacks against India occurred amid renewed efforts to reduce the long-standing tension between India and Pakistan and following a revitalised Indian engagement in Afghanistan. Again, the talk was postponed and India placed the ball squarely in Pakistan's court by keeping the communication channels open at various levels but also made it clear that India wanted to see action taken on terrorist attacks carried out against India, especially the Pathankot attack, the latest in the series. The Bangkok Mechanism (see below) worked as a damage control mechanism to revive the initiative, and the much awaited Comprehensive Bilateral Dialogue at Foreign Secretary level took place only on April 26, 2016. While Pakistan emphasised 'Kashmir' as the core issue[8] India utilised the platform to discuss a range of issues varying from trade to terrorism.

So far, Modi's foreign policy initiatives to Pakistan can be considered largely a 'personal diplomacy' executed with vigour, energy and enthusiasm. Though Modi adopted an 'out of the box' approach towards Pakistan, the new initiative failed due to certain reasons which are inherent in the Indo-Pak bilateral process.

Pakistan Army: A Peace-Breaker in Indo-Pak Bilateralism

A sequential detailing in the aforementioned paragraphs shows the Indian initiatives to improve its bilateral negotiations with Pakistan since 2014. It is to be noted that whenever the bilateral relationship is improving towards an active cooperation/engagement, the Pakistani military establishment produced a backlash in order to undermine the progress. The civilian governments' decision to engage each other through democratic dialogue has been challenged due to deep state involvement of Pakistan. This constant attempt of the Pakistan army to abort the democratic initiatives between both the states raises two major doubts regarding the credibility of Pakistan's civilian leadership to carry out an independent policy on India and on the feasibility of policy options adopted by the Indian diplomatic community. It is proved wrong that following bonhomie and rhetoric cannot influence the vested interests of the military establishment of Pakistan.

Diversification of Strategies

Since the first day in his office, Prime Minister Modi has been trying every possible way to reach out to Pakistan and negotiate to improve the relationship. Modi has won to diversify the diplomatic initiatives to engage Pakistan though the result has not scored well.

Personal Diplomacy

Using the clout of his personal diplomacy, Modi emerged successful in breaking the age-old practices in diplomacy. His initiatives to invite Pakistan's Prime Minister to attend the oath of office ceremony and subsequent discussion ignited a new start to the Indo-Pak bilateral relationship under the new government. Modi has never spared a chance to engage Pakistan whenever situations arose. Sideline talks were held between both the leaders during the BRICS meeting in 'Ufa', even after attempts were made to derail the process. Modi's surprise stopover in Lahore to wish his counterpart on his birthday while returning from Afghanistan was another warmth from the office of Indian Prime Minister to engage Pakistan. The Prime Minister has attracted criticism even from his own party men for his liberal approach towards Pakistan. But, Prime Minister Modi is also keen to stop Pakistan when Indian initiatives were jeopardised by terrorist attacks from Pakistan.

A Drive to Strengthen Sub-Regionalism

Materialisation of Bangladesh, Bhutan, India and Nepal (BBIN) Motor Vehicle Agreement for the Regulation of Passenger, Personal and Cargo Vehicular Traffic amongst BBIN, signed in November 2015, was a major accomplishment of Indian efforts to bring connectivity in the sub-region. The Agreement has been endorsed under special Indian interest to promote integration of the region. The Indian initiative to endure a sub-regional cooperation among smaller south Asian neighbours by actively engaging them and to create a 'zone of influence' will be a greater force to move together. The Agreement has been endorsed under special Indian interest to promote integration of the region. A framework agreement for Regional Agreement on Motor vehicle (RAM) was put in order during the 18th SAARC summit, but failed due to the indifference from Pakistan. By signing such an agreement, India demonstrated New Delhi's initiative to bring 'sub-regionalism' to counter Pakistan's move to derail integration and connectivity in the region. The strategy envisages fostering 'sub-regionalism minus Pakistan' to improve connectivity among SAARC states and pool support from other neighbours.

New Maritime Policy

Traditionally, India adopted a 'continental approach' in its foreign policy practices in general and towards Pakistan in special. Since the nature of challenges are being diversified and Indian peninsula is exposed to challenges from Bay of Bengal, Indian Ocean and Arabian Sea, there is no time to spare to formulate a rejuvenated maritime policy for India. China has already stolen the march over India in this region by its strategy called 'string of pearls'. By realizing India's strategic potentiality in Ocean region, Modi government seems to be looking for a revitalized maritime policy. The globalised world has necessitated greater cooperation between India and its littoral states, which is significant not only with regard to security affairs but also for economic prosperity of the region. Delhi's preparation to be equipped with a more purposeful engagement in Indian Ocean, project 'Mausam',[9] and evolving maritime 'Spice Route' projects are some significant foreign policy initiatives from the new government to counter Pak-China conglomeration by establishing both strategic and trade links with Indian Ocean littoral states. Project 'Mausam' envisages to re-establish India's link with its ancient trade partners, and this world would stretch from east Africa, along the Arabian peninsula, past southern Iran, to the major countries of South Asia and then to Sri Lanka and South East Asia. Modi government is keen to evolve a new maritime policy and explore the scope of the 'blue economy' so as to prepare India to tackle challenges from the 'Ocean world'. Modi's interest to strengthen 'the Indian Navy' exceeded expectations when the Prime Minister directed to organise 'Unified Commanders' Conference'—the crucial platform to discuss its national defence policy and operational challenges—onboard the INS *Vikramaditya*, about 50 km off Kochi.[10] This was for the first time in history that an annual tri-service meeting was being held outside the national capital. This signifies New Delhi's interest and investment in exploring a revitalized maritime policy.

Bangkok Mechanism

Bangkok Mechanism is the newly evolved dialogue platform represented by the national security advisors of India and Pakistan. This mechanism aims to improve engagement with security establishments and sharing information in case of terrorist attacks, and that would help to track down perpetrators through this channel to ensure timely action. Hence, it is learnt that India's National Security Advisor Ajit Doval has shared relevant information with his Pakistani counterpart on Pathankot attack leaving crucial decisions at Pakistan's end. Consequently, Pakistan's Joint Investigation Team visited Pathankot to collect evidence regarding Jaish-e-Mohammad's involvement in the attack. Though the response from Pakistan disappointed India, the platform helped to launch sharing of information with regard to threats from terrorism – the major challenge faced by both the states.

Defy Pak-China Axis

To defy the challenges posed by Pak-China axis in the region is one of the major tasks of India's foreign policy's course towards Pakistan. China and Pakistan are now self-declared "iron brothers" and "all-weather friends". The Sino-Pak nexus represents perhaps the most critical component of China's connection with the South Asian security environment. This has alarmed the Indian security establishments since the last five decades, and Modi was keen to address this security threat by opening both traditional and modern fronts of foreign policy engagement. Recent contribution from China to invest in energy and infrastructure[11] projects in Pakistan amounts to $46 billion. This monetary pledge is a part of China-Pakistan Economic Corridor. Financial and infrastructural support to Pakistan's Gwadar Port is an ambitious strategy of Beijing to open new routes rest of the world through Pakistan. And, Prime Minister Modi's visit to Iran in May 2016 has led to the much awaited signing of the pact to develop the strategic Chabahar Port in Iran,[12] which has been a fitting replay to this China-Pak axis. The port will make way for India to bypass Pakistan to access Afghanistan and Central Asia. At present Pakistan does not allow India to transport through its territory to Afghanistan. Modi's initiative to reaching out to 'neighbour's neighbour' is a strategic momentum with regard to India's Pak policy.

Embracing Formal Mechanism

After the flip-flop strategy fashioned by Prime Minister Modi during the 2014 and 2015 period, he has returned to embrace a conventional diplomatic style of formal and structured engagement with Pakistan after the Pathankot attack, realising the fact that Pathankot will not be the last one in this series. In April 2016, India and Pakistan decided to renew the dialogue process named Comprehensive Bilateral Dialogue (CBD), in which discussions would be carried over in a structured manner to address the prioritised issues. The CBD covers ten issues, including Kashmir, terrorism, trade and humanitarian issues.[13] This new approach comprises an inclusive strategy by sharing the concerns of both the states: for India terrorism is the top concern, but for Pakistan it is Kashmir. India's preference for promoting trade and transit route with Pakistan and Pak concern for Human Rights violations are also there on the card. The CBD also envisages addressing people-to-people contact and promoting religious tourism between India and Pakistan to improve the bilateral relationship. Bringing in the participation of civil society would be another affirmative step in this regard.

India's decision to continue engagement with Pakistan came from the realisation that non-engagement will not stop Pakistan from sponsoring terrorism. A structured but rejuvenated foreign policy initiative is the need of the hour to address Pakistan.

Prospects: Revisit the Existing Policy

A revitalised treatment is needed in India's policies towards Pakistan. Since India is looking forward to achieve long term strategic goals, India should adopt a policy which is a synthesis of diplomacy and defence/strategic traits. A revival of the existing policy can be possible if the following issues are addressed.

To Engage Pakistan's Military Establishment

Pakistan's military establishment, especially Pakistan Army, is the single most organized institution in that state. Since the formative days of Pakistan, the Army has controlled domestic as well as foreign policy making processes. Since the Pakistan army and its intelligence wing ISI are major stakeholders in Pakistan's 'India policy', it would be desirable to bring the Army to the discussion table, so that direct negotiation can be made possible with the institution which controls and formulates Pakistan's foreign and defence policies. Generally, the possibility of a direct negotiation with military establishment derives only when Pakistan falls under a military regime, otherwise the military establishment prefers to be behind the curtain. During the civilian rule, the Pakistan's military establishment used to appoint their surrogates as heads of different agencies/departments to exercise their control. Recent appointed a former general Naseer Khan Janjua as Pakistan's national security advisor[14] is an attempt to tighten military's control cover security policy and negotiations with India. The move shall be considered productive for India as it will help her to engage with a proxy of Pakistan's military establishment and apprehend their manoeuvre.

To Rejuvenate existing 'military doctrines'

A revision of existing military doctrines too is imminent to address the emerging challenges in the security sphere and revive effectiveness of 'retaliatory strikes' in case of an attack from the enemy land. The existing military doctrines viz. the 'Cold Start Doctrine'—though India has denied the existence of any such doctrines—proved slow in mobilising the forces at the time of crisis. Hence, a doctrinal practice which is fruitful in effective mobilisation and effective counter-retaliation would be apt for India to address the perpetrators of terrorism. 'Fear of retaliation' may be as effective as a 'retaliatory strike'. A revitalised military doctrine should be in tandem with 'modernization of military establishment and equipment', which would help to ensure that the counter 'retaliation' would hit on 'accurate target', so that any damage to the 'life and property' of civilians can be avoided.

Hence, India should espouse a policy which would be a combination of both 'civilian-democratic initiatives' and 'military-strategic initiatives'. The civilian-democratic initiatives may include bilateral diplomatic talks, trade talks and Track II diplomacy and 'military-strategic initiatives' like adopting a rejuvenated 'military doctrine' which would emphasise 'effective counter retaliation', starting negotiation on disputed territories like Kashmir, Sir Creek, etc. Since India is emerging as a leading power in the region, the state should also follow a democratic path to engage other states. Hence, adopting a stratagem which would be a combination of diplomatic engagements and defence policy would be apt to improve the bilateral relationship with Pakistan. India should diversify its strategies by evolving a new maritime policy to engage littoral states to defy increasing Pak-Chinese influence in the region and also start negotiating Pakistan's military establishment for productive outcomes.

REFERENCES

1. Concept of Continentalism is marked by an obsession with land frontiers and follow a sea blind policy. Scholars like C Raja Mohan argue that India's foreign policy priorities are predominantly influenced by this approach.
2. Narayanan, M K (2016), "The road from Pathankot", *The Hindu*, Chennai, 22 January, 2016.
3. Khan, Mubarak Zeb (2014) "Revival of Pak-India trade talks to be discussed next month", *The Dawn*, URL: http://www.dawn.com/news/1115812, accessed on 23 May 2016.
4. Haider, Suhasini (2014) "India, Pak Foreign secys to meet on 25 August", *The Hindu*, URL: http://www.thehindu.com/news/national/india-pak-foreign-secys-to-meet-on-aug-25/article6242148.ece, accessed on 27 May 2016.
5. "NSA appointment", *The Dawn*, URL: http://www.dawn.com/news/1215353, accessed on 6 June 2016,
6. "Modi meets Sharif on sidelines of Paris Climate Conference", *The Hindu*, URL: http://www.thehindu.com/news/national/modi-meets-sharif-on-sidelines-of-paris-climate-conference/article7933229.ece, accessed on 6 June 2016; Syyed, Baqir

Sajjad (2015) "Sharif meets Modi, 'exchange of courtesies or good talks?'", *The Dawn*, URL: http://www.dawn.com/news/1223472, accessed on 6 June 2016.

7. "Ghani Thunders, Swaraj Diplomatic at 'Heart of Asia Conference' in Capital", *The Dawn* URL: http://www.dawn.com/news/1225210, accessed on 10 June 2016.
8. "India-Pak Foreign Secretaries Meet; Pakistan reaffirms Kashmir as the core issue", *The Dawn*, URL: http://www.dawn.com/news/1254529, accessed on 10 June 2016.
9. Pillalamari, Akhilesh (2014) "Project Mausam: India's answer to China's 'Maritime Silk road'", *The Diplomat* , URL: http://thediplomat.com/2014/09/project-mausam-indias-answer-to-chinas-maritime-silk- road/, accessed on 27 May 2016.
10. "Modi chairs commanders' conference on board INS Vikramaditya", *Hindustan times*, URL: http://www.hindustantimes.com/india/kochi-modi-to-chair-commanders-conference-on-board-ins-vikramaditya/story-k1FvXM1qCJD11Ti2Dpp81N.html accessed on 15 July 2016.
11. Khan, Wajahat S (2016) "Gwadar Port Project Reveals China's Regional Power Play", URL: http://www.nbcnews.com/news/world/gwadar-port-project-reveals-chinas-regional-power-play-n558236, accessed on 15 July 2016.
12. 'India to develop Iran's Chahbahar Port', *The Hindu*, May 24, 2016.
13. Raja Mohan C (2016), "How Prime Minister Modi Can Sustain India's Pakistan Dialogue", Carnegie Endowment for International Peace, URL: http://carnegieendowment.org/2016/02/12/how-prime-minister-modi-can-sustain-india-s-pakistan-dialogue-pub-62707, accessed on June 28, 2016.
14. "Pakistan to appoint ex-general as new national security advisor", *The Hindu*, Chennai, 18 October 2015.

"Exclusive: Pakistan to appoint ex-general as new national security advisor", *Reuters*, July 2016,URL: http://www.reuters.com/article/us-pakistan-military-exclusive-idUSKCN0SC0TP20151018, accessed on 5 July 2016.

5

Revisiting India's Himalayan Neighbour: India's Contemporary Foreign Policy Initiatives towards Nepal

Nalini Kant Jha and K.R. Sreelekha

In its modern history, Nepal remained under absolute monarchy for a pretty long time; from the 1990s a transition to constitutional monarchy began and status quo remained until 2008. On September 20th Nepal adopted a new constitution envisaging a multi-party democracy under a federal republic. But, the adoption of the status as a 'Republic' is still under controversy, which casts doubt on the intention and capability of political parties to ratify and adopt the same on the floor of the legislature. The tiny kingdom of Nepal and its traditional monarchical rulers shared a cordial bilateral relationship with India in the past. But things began to change when there emerged a multi-party environment, which espoused for a greater role of Nepal in its regional context and freedom from Indian high-handiness in Nepal's domestic affairs.

Nepal is a small country landlocked between India and China; hence, the strategic significance of this country demands a special mention. Since the period of British imperialism, this state has been considered as a 'buffer state' between India and China. The complex security issues faced by this state vary from India to other neighbouring states in this region. Generally, both India and Nepal share relatively good bilateral relations, but occasional tense negations happen in terms of strategic security affairs, trade and transit route, water sharing and issues related to hydroelectricity generation, etc.

Security Concerns

Nepal, being a buffer state between two giant countries of the region, India and China, bears a significant position in the strategic security considerations of both the countries. Nepal is bordered by China to the north and India to the south, west and east. Nepal is separated from Bhutan by India's Sikkim and is separated from Bangladesh by a narrow corridor. Being close to Tibet, Nepal constitutes as a core concern for Chinese strategic designs too. The Chinese rail network to Tibet touching Nepal poses threats to India's security considerations in the region. Having already expanded its influence in Nepal with road and rail network through Tibet, China is now looking to stretch its railway link to Bihar to improve connectivity with India and South Asia.[1] A Wikileaks report shows that Pakistan intelligence agencies are targeting India through Nepal; the report reads that with the increased vigilance on the India–Pakistan border, the infiltration of the militants and the smuggling of arms across the Line of Control is becoming more and more difficult and risky. Nepal has therefore provided the ISI with an attractive second front.[2] Hence, a cordial relationship with Nepal became necessary for India.

Trade and Transit

Since Nepal is a landlocked country, for Nepal the nearest sea port is Kolkata in India; its dependence upon India for trade and transit route is relatively high. But the economic liberalisation undertaken by both countries brought fundamental changes in the pattern and direction of economic exchange between them.[3] India and Nepal signed a 'Treaty of Trade and Transit' in the year 1960 to facilitate a transit facility for Nepal; this treaty has been renewed periodically. But Nepal also witnessed indifferences from the Indian side to facilitate the transit routes when political differences with Nepal emerged. This has compelled Nepal to rely on China for alternative transit facilities, which led to flooding of Nepal's market with Chinese products.

Disputes on Water Resources

One of the major contentious issues in the India–Nepal bilateral relationship was the discord on water resources, tense negotiations relating to hydroelectricity generation, irrigation water and flood control.[4] The water sharing of major rivers originating in Nepal and flowing into India has strained the relationship between both the countries. Apart from this, scope for hydroelectricity generation is abundant for Nepal, but has lacked infrastructure facilities; if India can rectify this problem, India could buy the electricity produced in Nepal at a comparatively cheap price. This would explore new levels of bilateral relationship between both the states.

Apart from these issues, the open border, issues related with representation of *Madhesis* in Nepal, the constitutional crisis in Nepal are certain issues, on which both the countries find it difficult to move on. With the change of guard in New Delhi, the new government under the leadership of Narendra Modi, has been looking forward towards India's neighbourhood with an active Act East Policy, and that brings rays of hope in their bilateral relationship.

Modi's Endeavours in Nepal

Modi paid a visit to Nepal within three months of his accession to the Prime Ministership. Apart from the strategic significance of this tiny state, Modi liked to revive the socio-cultural and religious correspondence between India and Nepal. Modi believes that the strengthening of these religio-cultural factors would amplify the mutual course of action between both the countries. Modi is the first Indian Prime Minister to visit Nepal in 17 years, though there have been mutual exchanges of foreign ministers and ambassadors. Following are few relevant factors and issues which constitute prime concerns in Modi's foreign policy endeavours in Nepal.

Religio-Cultural Aspects

Prime Minister Narendra Modi was keen to promote religio-cultural linkages that exist between both India and Nepal and thereby reap the benefits. Upon his first visit to the Himalayan country Modi said that "my first visit reflects our shared heritage of nature, history, culture, spiritualism and religion. It highlights the high spirit that my government attaches to our relations with Nepal and our determination to take our relationship to an entirely new level".[5] Modi's visit to Pashupatinath temple in Nepal stimulated a sense of togetherness between the Hindu communities in both the countries. Sharing and caring of these religio-cultural elements would boost inter-state relationship and mutual cohesion. Prime Minister Modi employed this brilliant combination to reap befits for India. Asserting these religio-cultural linkages with Nepal will help India to claim that India would be meritorious than any other state to have a special relationship with Nepal.

Aid and Assistance

Prime Minister Narendra Modi addressed the Nepalese Parliament on August 2014; during his address he announced a 1 billion concessional line of credit to Nepal. He also mentioned that USD 1 million is in addition to any other existing Line of Credit (LoC).[6] In April 2015 Nepal was struck with the worst earthquake; within minutes of the earthquake, the Government of India sent the Indian Army for rescue, evacuation and relief work, and the initiative was named as *'Operation maitri'* (amity). Modi signed ten agreements with Nepal during his first visit in 2014 itself, which include infrastructure development and capacity building mechanisms. India will also build a police training academy in Nepal to train over 400 police officers annually.[7] His visit also resulted in flagging off the Delhi-Kathmandu bus services, which has been hailed by Modi to boost connectivity between the two countries.

Agreements on Hydroelectric Projects

Nepal is abundant with its water resources, though there are grey areas in water sharing between India and Nepal, and several early agreements about the shared projects have been controversial in Nepal. The present regime in India shows interest to fully explore this capacity of its neighbouring state so that both of them would benefit each other. Modi and his Nepalese counterpart inked an agreement on August 2014 to renew work on 5,600 MW Pancheshwar Multipurpose Project that will pave the way to start the stalled project. The two governments also signed an MoU regarding the amendment of Terms of Reference (ToR) of the Pancheshwar Multipurpose Project on the Mahakali river. Under the agreement, the two countries have agreed to move forward works relating to the Pancheshwar Development Authority by declaring the Pancheshwar authority regulation. The project falls under the integrated treaty on the Mahakali river, bordering both Nepal and India, which was signed in 1996. It could not be developed earlier as the two countries could not decide on the terms of reference.[8] On September 2014 on the sidelines of the 18th SAARC Summit, an Agreement was reached on Arun III between Investment Board Nepal and Satluj Jal Vidyut Nigam of India. Apart from this India also inked a Project Development Agreement (PDA) for the Upper Karnali Project that was signed on September 19, 2014 with the Govt. of Nepal;[9] the task to develop this project is assigned to the Indian infrastructure giant GMR. Thus within six months since being the Prime Minister, Modi injected over $ 3 billion of investments to Nepal till December 2014. In less than six months, since May 2014, Nepal has signed deals with India to build 1800 MW of hydropower- about triple the amount of electricity currently produced in the country.[10] Many people observe that it is Modi's diplomacy which fastens the deal with Nepal on such projects and Modi won to restore the idea that India is Nepal's most reliable hydropower ally.

Challenges in India's Nepal Policy

India's foreign policy course towards Nepal under the Prime Ministership of Narendra Modi until 2016 can be divided into two phases for analytical purposes. The first phase has been marked with an improved relationship and significant cooperation in the field of integration of the region and bilateral treaties but the second phase was marked with declining mutual trust, cooperation, allegation of interferences in Nepal's sovereignty, etc.

Constitutional Deadlock in Nepal and the Madeshi Issue

In September 2015, the Nepal Parliament passed the new constitution with 507 out of 601 members of its Constituent Assembly voting in favour.[11] The new charter replaces the interim constitution that governed the country since 2007. However, the Constitution has not been without controversy, as critics of the bill raised issue of lack of proper representation of Nepal's marginalizsed communities like the Tharu and Madheshi.

The new constitution has a provision for a 165-member parliament, but the constituencies have been demarcated in such a way that the people of the hill and the mountain region would get 100 seats, despite the fact that their share in Nepal's population is less than 50 per cent; because of the insensitivity shown towards the demands of Madheshi parties, a call was given by the unified Democratic Madheshi Front and Taruhat/ Thanruwan Joint Struggle Committee for an indefinite strike in Terai beginning on August 8, 2015.[12] The Madheshis and Tharus were sidelined in the entire constitution-making process due to the prevailing distrust towards them among the mainstream political parties.[13] Amidst these crises there were reports in favour of and against India's role in the blockade of the transit route to Nepal. Some argue that it is India's support to the

Madheshi issue and India's deliberate attempt to continue the blockade of the transit facility to Nepal, but there are others who argue that it is because of the fragile law and order situation in Nepal; the private trucks plying on the Indian side of the border cannot afford to cross the border and reach Nepal.

India also demanded a just representation of the Madheshi community; Indian worries on Nepal's constitution irritated Nepal's political parties and leadership, and resulted in stress and strain in the bilateral relationship between both the states for some time. Nepal expressed its disappointment and unhappiness with regard to Indian interference in Nepal's sovereignty. In March 2016, Nepal's Prime Minister K.P. Oli made a historic visit to China, which was an outcome of Nepal's initiatives to open more supply routes from China amid fears of the repeat of a recent nearly six-month long crippling blockade when the Indian-origin Madheshis blocked Nepal's trade routes with India, throwing normal life out of gear.[14] During his visit to China, Oli signed ten agreements with China, of which the most significant is an agreement by both countries on transit trade; by signing this treaty India's monopoly with regard to transit trade with Nepal came to an end. Nepal also expressed interest to be connected with China by connecting its rail link with Tibet. Nepal also signed a Free Trade Agreement to boost its trade relationship with China.

Thus, direct or indirect Indian involvement in Nepal's domestic affairs pulled India back from the age-old strategic hold which had been enjoyed by India in Nepal. The blockade of trade transit has invited China into the picture, which was keenly waiting for the right time to distract India's influence in Nepal. Along with China, now Pakistan has also signalled its willingness to have a trade relationship with Nepal. If this is going to materialise, that would be a strategic defeat for India in this region.

Controversies related to Water Resource Management

The controversies related to water sharing and management of water recourses are major areas of challenges faced by both India and Nepal. The Nepalese feel that they have not been treated equitably under the various water resources development agreements with India, including the Sarada, the Kosi and the Gandak. Nepal is also worried about India's river linking project. During the visit of Prime Minister Modi, he initiated to sign the Power Trading Treaty (PTA) which would allow transmission of electricity generated from Nepal's hydro projects to India, but Nepal is having apprehensions regarding India's monopoly on water sources and management of the same.

Easing of the Relationship

In January 2016, Nepal moved to amend several provisions of its constitution such as proportionate and inclusive representation of all marginalised communities including the Madheshis in all state mechanisms and allocation of seats in Parliament on the basis of population. This paved the way for easing tensions between India and Nepal as well as the Madheshis calling off their protests.[15] But the domestic political situation went wrong; following a move by the opposition parties (the Maoist and the Nepali Congress) to pursue a no-confidence motion on the floor of the Parliament, K.P. Oli, resigned from the post of Prime Minister and subsequently CPN-Maoist Centre Chief, Pushpa Kamal Dahal (Prachanda) was elected as the new Prime Minister, on August 4, 2016. In his second term Prachanda is cautious in framing his India policy; strategically he embraced both China and India simultaneously and attempts to balance both the powers.

India has also initiated far-reaching policies ranging from trade to tourism to improve the bilateral relationship between both the states. The signing of the BBIN Motor Vehicle Agreement and the hydroelectrical power cooperation agreements, the initiative of tackling water resource disputes—will have an abiding impact on India–Nepal relationship in the days to come.

REFERENCES

1. 'China looking to stretch Nepal rail link to Bihar : Report', *Indian Express*, 2016, URL: http://indianexpress.com/article/india/india-news-india/china-looking-to-stretch-nepal-rail-link-to-bihar-report-2816471/, (accessed August 2, 2016).
2. 'The Global intelligence Files, Files released 5543061', URL: https://wikileaks.org/gifiles/docs/65/65147_pakistan-intelligence-targeting-india-through-nepal-.html (accessed 3 August 2016).
3. Gyanu Raja Shrestha, Nepal-India Bilateral Trade Relations Problems and Prospect, p. 2. URL: http://www.ris.org.in/images/RIS_images/pdf/dp54_pap.pdf (accessed 5 August 2016).
4. Manadal, Monika, *Water Resources Cooperation between India and Nepal*, New Delhi: Knowledge World, 2016, p. x.
5. 'Prime Minister Narendra Modi enthralled Nepal by his visit', URL: http://www.narendramodi.in/prime-minister-shri-narendra-modi-enthralled-nepal-by-his-visit-6427 (accessed on 18 July 2016).

6. 'Modi concludes historic visit to Nepal', *The Times of India*, 2014. URL: http://timesofindia.indiatimes.com/india/Modi-concludes-historic-visit-to-Nepal/articleshow/39628843.cms (accessed on 5 August 2016).
7. 'PM Narendra Modi signs 10 agreements with Nepal, inaugurates bus service', *Times of India*, 2014, URL: http://timesofindia.indiatimes.com/india/PM-Narendra-Modi-signs-10-agreements-with-Nepal-inaugurates-bus-service/articleshow/45278008.cms (accessed on 8 August 2016).
8. 'India, Nepal Ink Three Pacts; Work on Pancheshwar Dam to Start Soon', *NDTV*, 2014, URL: http://www.ndtv.com/india-news/india-nepal-ink-three-pacts-work-on-pancheshwar-dam-to-start-soon-608593 (August 10, 2016).
9. GMR Upper Karnali Hydropower Limited, 900 MW HEP, Dailekh, Nepal, http://gmrgroup.in/energy-upper-karnali-project.aspx (accessed on 10 August 2016).
10. 'India and Nepal sign deal to build another mega-dam,' The third pole, 2014, URL: https://www.thethirdpole.net/2014/11/27/india-and-nepal-sign-deal-to-build-another-mega-dam/ (accessed on August 17, 2016).
11. Iyengar, Rishi, 'Nepal has finally passed a new constitution after years of political turmoil', URL: http://time.com/4037788/nepal-constitution-sushil-koirala-protests-madhesi-tharu/ (accessed on August 17, 2016).
12. Jha, Hari Bansh, 'Nepal's new constitution: An analysis from the Madheshi perspective', 2015, URL: http://www.idsa.in/idsacomments/NepalsNewConstitution_hbjha_240915 (accesed on 18 August 2016).
13. Ibid.
14. 'India's monopoly to end as Nepal gets trade point in China', *Times Now*, 2016, URL: http://indianexpress.com/article/world/world-news/nepal-signs-transit-agreement-with-china-to-get-first-railway-link/ (accessed on 24 August 2016).
15. Roche, Elizebeth, 'Narendra Modi, K.P. Oli meet in bid to push India-Nepal ties', 2016, http://www.livemint.com/Politics/aziBOp1zVIh9WO2A8SFfdI/Narendra-Modi-KP-Oli-discuss-IndiaNepal-ties.html (accessed on 24 August 2016).

6

Reaching out the Maritime World: Modi's Foreign Policy Initiatives towards Maldives

Nalini Kant Jha

Maldives is situated 400 km south-west of India and about 700 km south-west of Sri Lanka in the Indian Ocean. Maldives consists of about 1,190 islands, which spread over roughly 90,000 sq km.[1] It has a total population of 328,536, mainly dominated by Sunni Muslims. Non-Muslims cannot become citizens of Maldives.[2] Historically, the Maldives has remained a free nation, except during three occasions when it was ruled by outside forces. It was dominated by the Portuguese Empire for fifteen years in the mid-fifteenth century. In the mid-seventeenth century, the Dutch Empire (Malabar) dominated Maldives for four months. Finally, the Maldives became a British protectorate from 1887 until 1965.[3]

Maladies emerged as new republic on 11 November 1968 following a national referendum held on 15 March 1968, which ended the 853-year-old monarchy. Ibrahim Nasir became the first president of independent Maldives, remaining in office till 1978 when he resigned facing stiff political opposition. Subsequently, Maumoon Abdul Gayoom became the President in 1978 and stayed in office for the next three decades, during which he won six continuative presidential elections, but under a single-party, single-candidate format.[4] Gayoom's term witnessed a period of political stability and economic prosperity. He was in fact credited for transforming the

Maldives into a destination for high-end, high-value resort-tourism. He also strengthened the Maldives' relations with other countries. At the same time, Gayoom was equally criticised for his totalitarian behaviour. He suppressed his political opponents by limiting freedoms and a resort to political favouritism.[5] Faced with political protests in 2004 and 2005, the Maldives under President Gayoom underwent a series of political reforms. This finally resulted in the drafting of a third Republican Constitution in 2007, and fresh elections to the presidency took place in 2008, in which Mohamed Nasheed emerged as the winner, becoming the first President of the Maldives under the multi-party format. This was held as "heralding a new era of democracy and progressive politics".[6]

In fact, the people started expecting that with the new Constitution in place and with Nasheed as the President Maldives would further successfully march towards deepening of democratic transition in the country, which in turn will make the people exercise real freedom for which they had been struggling for years. However, all these expectations were dashed to the ground just three years after the coming of the new Constitution into existence. In a surprising move Nasheed resigned on February 7, 2012, leading to another spell of political uncertainty and turmoil in Maldives.[7] Nasheed claimed that he was threatened with a "bloodbath" if he refused to step down. In his address to the nation soon after his resignation, Nasheed stated, "I don't want to hurt any Maldivian. I feel my staying on in power will only increase the problems, and it will hurt our citizens. So the best option available to me is to step down".[8] Yet, Mohammad Waheed Hassan Manik, who took over as President, insisted that it was "not a coup". Political dismay and opportunistic alliances continued in Maldives resulted in regimes with short span of life. One such incident led to the emergence of Abdulla Yameen of Progressive Party of Male, as the new President after the election held on 2013 (continuing).

A Background to the Contemporary Political Stalemate

The toppling of the Nasheed regime and cancellation of contract with Indian infrastructure developer GMR strained India's relations with Maldives since 2012. Despite the election of Nasheed as President through a multi-party democratic process, there had been attempts to destabilise and topple his regime. For instance, when Nasheed concentrated on freedom, independence of judiciary and anti-corruption to make Maldives as "the most promising young democracy in the region," the Majlis, Maldives' Parliament, dominated by the opposition Dhivehi Rayyithunge Party (DRP) (party of Nasheed's predecessor Abdul Gayoom) and its allies did not offer required cooperation, resulting in frequent political and constitutional deadlocks. Rather, parties like PPM, the conservative Islamic formations, the Adhaalath Party and Dhivehi Quamee Party (DQP) and Dhivehi Rayyithunge Party (DRP), along with other Islamist non-governmental organisations joined hands in what they called as the 'Coalition of 23rd December' to oust Nasheed.[9] They started agitations and protests against his alleged 'un-Islamic acts, corruption, autocratic functioning and mal-governance'. They also blamed him for violation of the Constitution and for his proximity to Israel. In a surprising move on the night of January 29 they met the then Vice-President Waheed to request him to take over the functions of Presidency and called upon the MNDF and the Maldivian police force to defy Nasheed and instead, pledge allegiance to Waheed.[10] Vice-President Waheed was reported to have agreed to all the terms proposed by the 'December 23 Coalition' which presumably included rehabilitating Gayoom protégés back in power under Waheed's leadership.[11]

Maldives' stagnant economy also played an important role in ousting Nasheed. Unemployment and high inflation damaged Nasheed's popular standing as well. The President was left with no option but to embark on major fiscal and economic reforms overseen by the International Monitory Fund (IMF). The structural reforms involved curtailing of State spending, while freeing the private sector to make it the engine of growth, in addition to devaluation of rufiyaa. In the present political crisis Islamic radicals also played an important role. There has been growing Islamic radicalism in Maldives. Islamic radicals have been trying to create problems for the Government of Nasheed who represented the moderate stream in the country. The country plunged into a constitutional crisis when Nasheed ordered the arrest of the Chief Criminal Judge Abdulla Mohamed in a joint operation by the police and Maldives National Defence Force (MNDF) on January 16. Due to the mishandling of the situation a political stand-off with religious overtones was transformed into an impasse between his Government and the judiciary, which prompted many of his supporters to desert him. Nasheed's mishandling of the situation precipitated the crisis resulting in his ouster.

The situation in Maldives worsened further when an arrest warrant was issued against Nasheed for illegally detaining Chief Criminal Court Judge Abdulla Mohamed during his final days in office. The political turmoil reached an alarming point and received the attention of the world community at one point of time when Nasheed sought refuge in the Indian Embassy in Male to escape the arrest warrant. Though he came out of the Indian Embassy only when a deal reportedly took place that he would not be arrested and will not be prevented from contesting the presidential elections, Nasheed was arrested within a fortnight after he left the Indian High Commission. This in turn clearly reflects the fact that Maldives is in a severe political crisis and the democratic process that started in 2008 with a new constitution has received a major jolt, pushing Maldives further in a backward direction.

Relations between India and Maldives became very acrimonious when Waheed cancelled the contract signed with GMR, an Indian company that was given a lucrative contract to renovate and run for 25 years, Male's only international airport.[12] Thus, when Waheed wanted to visit India, New Delhi sent a strong signal to Maldives that India is not willing to engage with its current leadership after the GMR controversy; the government has turned down an official request from the Maldivian foreign minister to visit India to set up a visit by the Maldivian president. And there is now some acceptance that Waheed is really the '*mukhauta*' or mask of former dictator Maumoon Abdul Gayoom, who is running the show from behind the scenes.

Subsequently, Former Maldives President Gayoom, who visited India in June 2013 on the invitation of Prime Minister Manmohan Singh, tried to iron out the differences with India by saying that the PPM government would talk to any Indian investor including GMR. In fact, he blamed President Mohamed Nasheed for inking a faulty contract with GMR that resulted in its termination. The Indian foreign policy establishment views this as a significant step forward towards addressing the present impasse between the two countries.[13]

Changing Contours of Maldivian Politics

It is feasible to analyse India's contemporary engagement with Maldives on the basis of the following factors:

(a) current strategic significance of the region viz. Maldives

(b) increasing Chinese influence in the region
(c) intensification of Islamic adherence and lenience towards Saudi Arabia and Pakistan

Today, Maldives has emerged as one of the most important neighbours of India in the geostrategic and economic terms. For, Maldives is located south of India's Lakshadweep Islands in the Indian Ocean, covering 820 km long and 120 km wide spread of the strategic Indian Ocean.[14] In turn, its geographical location makes it very important for India because it is situated mid-way between the Strait of Malacca and Suez, which are the world's busiest trade routes and thousands of cargoes pass through these two trade routes. At the same time, as the state of Kerala and the union territory of Lakshadweep are in close proximity to the Maldivian islands, there are always India's concerns about the possible use of Maldives' territory against it. These concerns get importance in the light of the fact that the November 2008 cross-border terrorist attack in Mumbai was made possible from across the sea. There are already reports that Pakistan's notorious terrorist outfit, Lashkar-e-Toiba was seeking a foothold in the Maldives by exploiting the Islamic connection.[15] Maldives also occupies a special place in India's foreign policy priority list because of special focus on this region by the US under its pivot towards Asia policy on the one hand, and on the other hand increasing cases of piracy in the Indian Ocean near Somalia and Strait of Malacca; this made the position of Maldives very important for establishing naval bases for security in the Indian Ocean.

A detailed description of the facts and analysis in the aforementioned paragraphs clearly reveals the strategic significance of the region in the contemporary international system. Reports on Chinese infrastructure investment for the port developments in Maldives raised concerns in India. Another contentious step from Maldives, which irked India was that after the termination of contract with Indian infrastructure tycoon GMR, Maldives signed a deal with a Chinese company to upgrade its international airport on September 2014 during the visit of Chinese President Xi Jinping.[16] The security agencies here have repeatedly been saying that the Marao Island which was leased by Maldives to China in 1999 for maritime traffic management was also being used by the Chinese to monitor Indian and US warships in the Indian Ocean, and in future could be developed into a submarine base.[17] On July 23, 2015, Abdulla Yameen, the President of Maldives approved a law allowing foreign ownership of land in the country for the first time, triggering concern in New Delhi over a possible opportunity for China to extend its reach in the Indian Ocean region.[18] These issues have sharpened the regional competition for influence in Indian Ocean Region.

Ever since the new regime of Abdulla Yameen took charge in November 2013, the island was moving on par with religious conservatism and leniency towards Sunni Islam. The Ministry of Islamic affairs has began to prioritise its policies on par with Islamic ideologies and which include blocking all religions except Islam in the nation, ensuring that all the laws and regulations adhere to Islamic principles and indulging in promoting institutions to strengthen Islamic fatwas to regulate the society and polity. In a changing strategic context Maldives was trying to engage extensively with Saudi Arabia and Pakistan; Saudi Arabia has already promised the Maldives a five-year soft loan facility of $300m (£181m)[19] in 2013 itself, and there was a manifold increase in Saudi Arabian investment in Maldives by 2015. The country is also seeking Saudi partnerships in energy and transport, but the biggest cooperation sector is Islamic affairs; the Saudi Prince has pledged to build ten "world-class" mosques in the archipelago, seven of them this year, while visiting Saudi scholars recently pledged a grant of $100,000 for Islamic education.[20] During his visit to Pakistan on May 7, 2015, Maldives' President expressed immense importance to its bilateral relationship with Pakistan. The Maldivian President's visit had taken place immediately after the arrest and trial of former President Mohamed Nasheed and the toppling of his democratic government, and raised doubts and disappointment among many states including India.

The radicalisation of Maldivian society created an environment where allegiance and adherence to terrorism and violent extremism are seen at a visible rate. There are reports on Maldivians leaving their homeland for joining the IS. President Abdulla Yameen submitted the paper for parliamentary debate last week; Yameen has been accused of ignoring the threat posed by jihadi recruitment since the first reports of Maldivians joining militant groups emerged two years ago. The opposition claims as many as 250 Maldivians are fighting in Syria and Iraq – the highest number in the region.[21]

India's engagement to Maldives has been in a suspended mode since the toppling of the then President Mohamad Nasheed in 2012. But the aforesaid developments and changing strategic environment compelled India to adopt a pragmatic policy with regard to Maldives.

Modi Saga on Maldives

By embracing an articulated foreign policy option called "neighbours first", Prime Minister Narendra Modi rejuvenated India's stalled policy initiatives towards Maldives. Chinese encirclement of India Ocean, increasing influence of Pakistan and *Wahhabi Islam* in Maldives propelled the Indian leader to revive the policy options.

The Modi regime has shown a little delay in resuming its relations with Maldives, which was stagnated due to domestic unrest following the arrest of former Maldivian President Mohamad Nasheed. This archipelago nation had been omitted from the list of four-nation Indian Ocean tour of Modi in March 2015; the government of Mohamed Yameen was disappointed over the cancellation of Modi's visit and its political implication. India's move has been articulated as its disparagement on Maldivian developments. But, the Modi government was fast to recover from the scratch, by paying a high level visit to Maldives by the External Affairs Minister Sushma Swaraj. She co-chaired and revived the scope of Indo-Maldives Joint Commission; the joint commission was meeting after a gap of 15 years.[22] A revival plan of the joint commission also aims to broaden its emphasis by including defence and security related issues.[23] Upon India's 'neighbours first policy', Maldivian President Yameen reiterated Maldives policy of 'India first'.

Barring the initial stagnation in Modi government's reach-out to Maldives, the subsequent developments starting from the annual joint military exercise "Ekuverin 2015" held from 31 August to 13 September, a high level visit paid by Swaraj on October 2015 and efforts of the Indo-Maldives Joint Commission to deal with security and defence issues show that security and defence constitute primary concerns of Indian engagement in Maldives. As a corollary to these initiatives, the Maldivian president paid a two-day visit to India on April 2016. This action plan envisages an institutional mechanism at the level of the Defence Secretaries to further the bilateral defence cooperation. In addition to defence and security collaborations, both the states agreed to improve cooperation in the fields of tourism, joint research and exploratory surveys in Maldives, avoidance of double taxation, etc.

Apart from security concerns and growing leniency towards Islamic fundamentalism, it is authoritarianism and the undemocratic nature of the present government which aggravate India's worry with regard to

Maldives. A 'democratic and sovereign neighbour' is one of the preconditions for peaceful co-existence and development of a region; hence India was anxious about the toppling of a democratic regime under Mohamed Nasheed. There were repeated appeals from former Maldivian President Mohamed Nasheed to India that "to stop appeasing dictators (the present regime) and India can play an important role in the restoration of democracy in the Maldives".[24] The Maldivian President drew international criticism since November 2015 after he declared national emergency and repression of his political opposition to a large extent. An extra-ordinary meeting of Commonwealth Ministerial Action Group (CMAG) held on February 25, 2016, called upon the Maldives and urged the government to initiate inclusive national political dialogue; the forum also expressed its continuing concern regarding the political space available to the opposition; the Ministerial Action Group also called for a free and fair election by 2018.[25] Upon the deliberation of the Commonwealth Ministerial Action Group meeting, India protected the Maldivian government against a possible punitive action from this forum. Pakistan also extended its support to Maldives with regard to this issue. This move of India in extending its support to Maldives has invited criticism from across the international community. Immediately after this incident the Maldivian President paid a visit to India on April 2016, and thanked India for 'protecting' his country from a possible punitive actions from CMAG, which had been asking Maldives to move towards genuine democracy.[26]

The decision of Modi government to engage Maldives demonstrates the pragmatic dimension of foreign policy initiative of his government. A revival of India's foreign policy initiatives towards Maldives has made some result oriented changes in this regard. Maldivian government's reciprocity towards Indian initiatives substantiate India's stance on this issue.

India's Concern in the Indian Ocean

India is a major continental power with strong maritime interest, especially in the Indian Ocean Region. The exploration of this region through different strategic and economic fora like Indian Ocean Rim Association (IORA), Bay of Bengal Initiative for Multi-Sectoral Technical and Economic Cooperation (BIMSTEC) and Indian Ocean Naval Symposium (IONS), etc., reveals the strategic significance of this region. The importance of the

Indian Ocean was highlighted by the American strategist Robert D. Kaplan. According to him, the Indian Ocean area will be the true nexus of world power and conflict in the coming years, it is here that the fight for democracy, energy, independence and religious freedom would be lost or won.[27] The importance of the Indian Ocean is so significant that the Sea Lanes of Communication (SLOCs) pass through it. A major part of the world's seaborne trade takes place through them. The energy resources required by the world's major economies pass through them. Moreover, the important centres of production of oil and gas – both offshore and onshore – are located around it. Besides, this region is also rich in fisheries and undersea minerals. These resources, in particular oil and gas reserves, have aroused and maintained the interest of the world's major and upcoming powers for their economic and strategic value.[28]

One of the foremost writers to who expressed the Indian perspective on the Indian Ocean and sea power was K.M. Panikkar. According to him, the "importance of the sea came to be recognised by the Indian rulers only when it was too late".[29] When India realised the strategic significance of this region, the other world powers, especially China, had already gained monumental achievement in this region. India is yet to fully explore the possibilities of this region viz. Maldives.

The Prospects

Regarding the bilateral cooperation with the Maldives, strategic security and defence predominate all other concerns; this is especially because of the geostrategic location of this archipelago nation. The need of the hour demands India shall play a pro-active role towards this island nation though it is a tiny piece of land. Intensification of Chinese presence over this island nation has stolen the march of India in this region. An active engagement with Maldivian leadership with pragmatism is the feasible option for India. Diversification in the field of bilateral engagement is a propitious move that India can adopt at this juncture of time in order to reap the benefit.

REFERENCES

1. http://en.wikipedia.org/wiki/Maldives (accessed on March 08, 2013).
2. https://www.cia.gov/library/publications/the-world-factbook/geos/mv.html (accessed on March 08, 2013).

3. n. 4
4. 'The Maldives: mired in presidential intrigue', http://www.aljazeera.com/indepth/features/2012/09/20120116544631 (accessed on March 09, 2013).
5. http://articles.cnn.com/2008-11- 11/world/maldives.president_1_sea-levels... (accessed on March 09, 2013).
6. 'Maldives presidential elections, 2008', http://en.wikipedia.org/wiki/Maldivian_presidential_election,_2008 [accessed on March 12, 2013]. Also see, Anand Kumar, 'A Year of Multi-Party Democracy in Maldives', Institute for Defence Studies and Analyses, http://www.idsa.in/issuebrief/AYearofMulti-PartyDemocracyinMaldives_akumar_060410 (accessed on March 13, 2013).
7. Yameen Rasheed, 'The Maldives: big stakes for India', in Sharmila Joshi (ed), *Neighbourhood Views of India*, New Delhi: Indian Council of Global Relations, 2012, pp. 44-57.
8. *BBC News Asia*, 2012, http://www.bbc.co.uk/news/world-asia- 16945764?print=true (accessed on March 09, 2013)
9. S D Muni, 'Stabilising the neighbourhood?: India's flip flop approach to Maldives crisis', ISAS Working Paper, 2012, no. 145-16,
10. BBC News Asia, February 08, 2012, http://www.bbc.co.uk/news/world-asia-16945764?print=true (accessed on March 09, 2013).
11. 'Vice president agreed to all terms proposed: December 23 coalition', *Haveeru online*, January 31, 2012, http://www.haveeru.com.mv/news/40026 (accessed on March 10, 2013).
12. Malhotra, Inder, 'India's Maldivian mess has not ended', http://www.viewpointonline.net/indias-maldivian- mess-hasnt- (accessed on March 10, 2013).
13. http://articles.economictimes.indiatimes.com/2013-04-15/news/38556162_1_senior-maldivian- minister-india- and-maldives-defence-minister (accessed on March 10, 2013).
14. Anand Kumar, 'Maldives harmonising efforts to mitigate adverse impacts of climate change and achieve growth', in Rumel Dahiya and Ashok K. Behuria (eds), *India's Neighbourhood: Challenges in the Next Two Decades*, New Delhi: Pentagon Press, 2012, pp. 110-136.
15. Muni, n. 12
16. 'Maldives allows foreign ownership of land despite opposition concern', *the Reuters*, 2015, http://in.reuters.com/article/maldives-land-foreigners-idINKCN0PX1FI20150723 (accessed on August 23, 2016).
17. 'Ties with China very close, far more precious with India: Maldives President', January 5, 2014, dnaindia, http://www.dnaindia.com/world/report-ties-with-china-very-close-far-more-precious-with-india-maldives-president-1945682 (accessed on August 12, 2016).
18. 'Maldives law selling foreigners islands stokes Delhi's fears of rising Chinese role', *The Guardian*, 2015 (accessed on August 28, 2016).
19. 'Saudi Arabia's growing role in the Maldives', Charles Haviland, BBC News, Colombo, March 24, 2014, http://www.bbc.com/news/business-26668107 (accessed on August 23, 2016).

20. Ibid.
21. Naish, Ahmed 'Government unveils 'zero tolerance' counter-terrorism policy', Maldives Independent, 2016, http://maldivesindependent.com/politics/government-unveils-zero-tolerance-counter-terrorism-policy-124856 (accessed on June 17, 2016).
22. Embassy of India, Male, Website, 2016, http://www.hci.gov.in/male/?4570?000 (accessed on June 17, 2016)
23. Ibid.
24. 'Maldives is sitting on a time bomb', March 4, 2016, *The Hindu*.
25. 'Extraordinary Meeting of the Commonwealth Ministerial Action Group Concluding Statement', February 24, 2016, www. the commonwealth.org: http://thecommonwealth.org/media/news/extraordinary-meeting-commonwealth-ministerial-action-group-concluding-statement#sthash.4Ps0Z4pb.dpuf (accessed on July 4,2016).
26. 'Maldives Thanks India for support', *The Hindu*, April 12, 2016.
27. Kumar, Anand, 'Multi party democracy in the Maldives and the emerging security environment in the Indian Ocean Region democracy maldives', IDSA, New Delhi: Pentagon Press, p. 95.
28. Ibid, p. 97.
29. Ibid, p. 96.

7

India and Bhutan: A Classic Example of a Symbiotic Relation

Shivaraju C.D.

Introduction

India's historic linkages with Bhutan are centuries old, and it is just not geography that connects these two countries, their societies have been enriched by links of culture and commerce over a period of time. "My inner voice said that my first foreign visit as the Prime Minister of India should be to Bhutan" said Prime Minister Narendra Modi for choosing Bhutan as the first foreign destination during his two-day visit to Thimpu in June 2014. However, the civilisational, economic and geostrategic significance were the guiding forces behind his visit which urged to revitalise this 'special relationship' enjoyed by India and Bhutan. Similarly, all-weather neighbourhood and friendship between the world's largest and youngest democracies resulted into an organic relationship. Indeed, this exemplary relationship is testimony to India's proactive responses to its neighbourhood and evolved over a span of time through mutual and mature understanding. Interestingly, the relationship between Thimpu and New Delhi can be termed as symbiotic because India has never considered Bhutan as a burden, rather beneficial to each other's growth and security. Thus, scholars have pointed out that India and Bhutan are natural allies. In other words, they are made for each other or Bharat for Bhutan (B4B) and vice versa. Furthermore, efforts have been made to retain the same mutual trust and confidence by recalling the historical relations and recognising with deep satisfaction a further enhancement of political and economic engagements.

Geostrategic Imperatives

Bhutan is considered as a buffer zone between the world's most populous and rapidly emerging economies, and gains significance primarily for strategic reasons. Thus, its geographical position is equally important for New Delhi and Beijing.

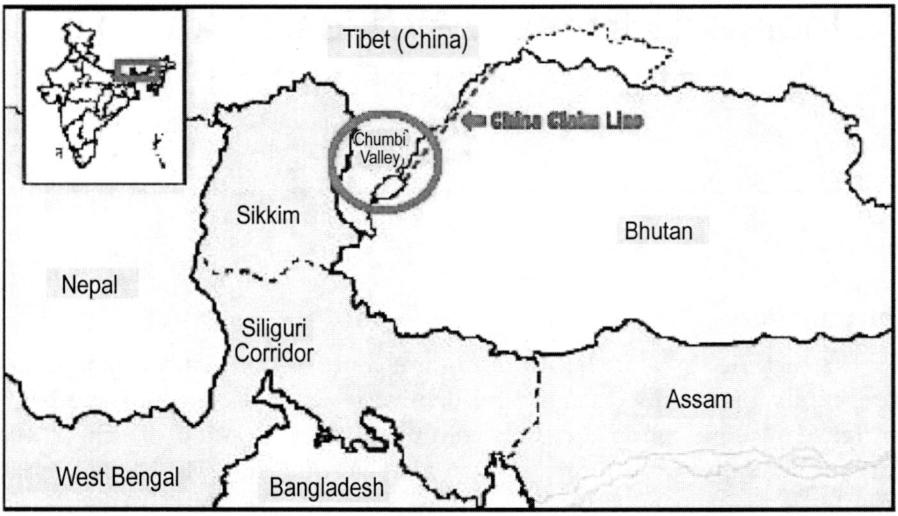

Disputed areas between Bhutan and China

Map courtesy: (Yesheydorji.blogspot.in)

There are three territorial disputes between China and Bhutan. China is making all the efforts to lay its footprint in these areas: they are the Jakarlung and Pasamlung valleys on the Bhutan–China north-central border, and the Doklam plateau in eastern Bhutan. The main reasons for its assertiveness are historical and geographical proximity to Tibet which will eventually have spillover effect on India. India's Centre for Land Warfare Studies (CLAWS) aptly describes the strategic value of the region: "The Doklam Plateau lies immediately east of Indian defenses in Sikkim. Chinese occupation of Doklam would turn the flank of Indian defenses completely. This piece of dominating ground not only has a commanding view of the Chumbi Valley but also overlooks the Siliguri Corridor further to the east". It also warns that the Siliguri Corridor also known as Chicken's Neck is a narrow stretch of land that connects India's north-eastern states to the rest of India. If the Chinese were to gain possession of the Doklam plateau, in the event of hostilities it would have the ability to "cut-off" India's land access to 40 million citizens in its north-east territories. At the same time, this landlocked country is also vital for India's security and development reasons. In an effort to combat insurgency and ensure development in the north-eastern states, the cooperation of Bhutan plays a major role. On the other hand, formal diplomatic relations and a diplomatic mission are yet be established between China and Bhutan. However, China is making all the efforts with Bhutan to have a 'comprehensive solution' to sort out border problems as early as possible in the name of fair and reasonable solutions. Nevertheless, it is interesting to know that even during the Sino-Indian War of 1962 Bhutan adopted a policy of neutrality towards China, while quietly expanding its relations with India as it was more fearful of China's strength than India's ability to defend. Thus, as pointed out by former Foreign Secretary Sujatha Singh, "Bhutan is one of our most important strategic partners...It is a very good country to show our policy of good neighbourliness in South Asia and special token of our friendship".[1]

Historical and Cultural Linkages

The formal diplomatic relations between India and Bhutan were established in 1968. However, the Treaty of Friendship and Cooperation signed in 1949[2] and renewed during His Majesty Jigme Khesar Namgyel Wangchuck's visit to India in February 2007 has been a guiding force as well as foundation for both countries' relations, as it emphasises perpetual peace and friendship, free trade and commerce and equal justice to each other's citizens. As a result, this traditional and unique relation, characterised by mutual trust and understanding evolved and got maturity over a period of time. Interestingly, His Majesty Jigme Khesar Namgyal Wangchuck, the King of Bhutan and the Queen visited India as the Chief Guest on the 64th Republic Day celebrations in 2013.[3] On the other hand, India is promoting democracy by formulating election laws and conducting elections. India provided a grant of Rs 47.506 million to the Royal Government of Bhutan to source electronic voting machines from India.[4] Further, the managerial support under the delegation of former Chief Election Commissioners of India Navin Chawla, Dr S.Y. Quraishi and V.S. Sampath was extended for a smooth and hassle-free election as well as the promotion of good electoral practices in the region. Hence, India has put in all the efforts for a peaceful transition of Bhutan from monarchy to democracy. Additionally, the regular high level political interactions are equally contributing for further strengthening ties between two. Similarly, there is a close bilateral cooperation in the educational and cultural fields between India and Bhutan. In fact, schemes such as the Nehru Wangchuck Scholarship and Bhutan-ICCR Scholarship[5] have provided golden opportunities to more than 100 Bhutanese students who are at undergraduate and postgraduate levels to pursue their higher learning in the Indian educational institutions. Besides, nearly 3,000 Bhutanese students have benefited from the Ambassador's Scholarship programme along with ten slots in Sainik Schools from class 6th to 12th standard. The Nehru-Wangchuck Cultural Centre and India-Bhutan Foundation contribution in enhancing people-to-people contact focusing on areas such as education, culture and environment protection is remarkable. Thus, "Our relations with Bhutan are unique and especially warm. Our historical and cultural linkages make us natural friends and partners" as observed by the former Foreign Secretary Sujatha Singh.

Clean and Green Energy Ties

The Land of Thunder is also blessed with fast-flowing and perennial rivers. The Drangme Chhu, the Puna Tsang Chhu or Sankosh, the Wang Chhu, and the Torsa Chhu are the major river systems of the Bhutan which ultimately drain into the Brahmaputra river of India.[6] Thus, they are considered as the 'power house' of Bhutan as they generate a huge amount of hydroelectricity which constitutes a major part of its economy. In other words, hydroelectricity is the backbone of Bhutan's economy because hydropower exports provide more than 40% of Bhutan's revenues, and constitute 25% of its GDP.[7] Besides, 25% contribution to the GDP comes from hydropower infrastructure construction. Technically, Bhutan is home to green and clean energy with potential of about 30,000 MW of which, 24,000 MW is technically feasible and economically viable.[8]

It is interesting to know that India consumes nearly 75% electricity generated in Bhutan at a reasonable rate. So, Bhutan has become an evergreen energy partner in India's growth story by meeting the growing energy demand. In fact, it is Bhutan's surplus and India's scarcity of energy which further strengthened the energy ties. Thus, much of finance and technical effort has been invested in the hydropower and related sectors. Three major projects have been signed in an Inter-governmental agreement (IG) between India and Bhutan and include:[9]

Table 1

Power Project	*Capacity*	*River*
Nikachhu	118-MW	At the confluence of the Nikachhu and Chhunabachhu
Rothpashong	1,125-MW	Kurichhu
Dagachhu	126-MW	Dagachhu

Additionally, four joint venture efforts have been also made to increase the generating capacity of the hydroelectric projects. They mainly constitute:

Table 2

Power Project	*Capacity*	*River*
Kholongchhu	600-MW	Kholongchhu
Wangchhu	570-MW	Wangchhu
Bunakha	180-MW	Wangchhu
Chamkharchhu	770-MW	Chamkharchhu

Furthermore, according to the 2009 protocol to the 2006 Bhutan-India Agreement, New Delhi has to provide grants and soft loans to Thimpu to produce 10,000 MW by 2020 and import all the surplus electricity. This effort will be a remarkable milestone once these projects commissioned through India's ambitious efforts result in an undisrupted energy flow.

Similarly, Bhutan being a landlocked country covered by mountainous terrain is largely depending on India not only for monetary but also skilled manpower assistance to have a robust infrastructure. On the other hand, the South Asia Association for Regional Cooperation is also showing a keen interest to implement the framework for inter-regional grid connectivity cooperation to harness the full potential of hydroelectric capacity of Bhutan in mitigating the energy drought of the region. However, climate change and global warming are big hurdles in reaping full potential of the sustainable energy source along with inbuilt geological problems. Despite the difficulty, China is in the forefront to lay its footprints in Bhutan both in terms of monetary and technical aid.

Major Development Partners

Despite the geopolitical complexities and security challenges, India and Bhutan are interdependent for economic prosperity with the seamless flow of goods, services, capital and people. Thimpu is a productive partner in building strong trade, transport, energy, digital and people-to-people links. The Treaty of Friendship 1949, calling for peace between the two nations also established a free trade and extradition protocol. Bhutan is a major economic and trading partner of India, as 91% of its exports and 82% of imports are from India. New Delhi is a vital donor of economic aid to Bhutan, as nearly 70% of the total foreign assistance goes from India. In fact, all the financial aid from India to Bhutan includes 60% of its budget. The following table gives the export and import picture between India and Bhutan.[10]

Table 3

Particulars	*2009*	*2010*	*2011*	*2012*	*2013*	*2014*
Exports to Bhutan (Imports from India) (Rs. Cr)	1984	2930	3520	4180	4389	47.85
Exports to Bhutan from India as a % to total Bhutanese import	77.7%	75.1%	72.3%	79.4%	82.4%	89.31%
Imports from Bhutan (Exports to India) (Rs. Cr)	2241	2600	2640	2780	2898	3180
Imports from Bhutan to India as a % to total Bhutanese export	93.5%	88.7%	83.8%	93.9%	91%	89.38%

Curiously, Bhutan followed India's model in development by launching the Five Year Plan in 1961. Since then, India is a principal contributor to the socio-economic development of Bhutan. In fact, India extended 100% financial assistance during the First and Second Five Year Plans. Similarly, India remained as a major donor by offering Rs 5,000 crore in the 10th FYP and Rs 4500 Crore in the 11th FYP. The following table depicts India's continues financial assistance to Bhutan since the launching of the FYP.[11]

Table 4

Year	*Total Allocations*	*India's Contribution*	*India's Contribution (%)*
1961-66 [1st Plan]	10.72	10.72	100
1966-71 [2nd Plan]	20.22	20.22	100
1971-76 [3rd Plan]	47.52	42.66	90.00
1976-81 [4th Plan]	110.62	85.30	77.00
1981-87 [5th Plan]	444.05	134.00	30.2
1987-92 [6th Plan]	950.00	400.00	42.1
1992-97 [7th Plan]	2350.00	750.00	31.9
1997-2002 [8th Plan]	4000.00	1050.00	26.00
2002-08 [9th Plan]	8900.00	2610.14	29.33
2008-13 [10th Plan]	14900.00	3400.00*	23.00
2013-18 [11th Plan]	21300.00	4500.00	21.00

* Excludes our assistance towards mega projects.

Additionally, the Government of India agreed to provide Rs. 500 Crore as Economic Stimulus Package to help the Royal Government of Bhutan to tackle the liquidity shortage. Similarly, India has generously deployed funds and expertise for an entire array of landmark projects, including the airport at Paro, the Bhutan Broadcasting Station, the Bhutan-India microwave link, one million-tonne Dungsum Cement Plant and the Bhutan Institute of Medical Sciences. Importantly, Modi has referred to Bhutan's unique trait of laying thrust on 'Gross National Happiness' (GNH) rather than Gross Domestic Product (GDP); parameters for measuring this could be the consideration that it has a neighbour like India.[12] At the same time, Bhutan as a growing economy is also interested to take an economic pilgrimage before spiritual pilgrimage, thus it seeks full cooperation and assistance from India in the matter of trade and commerce. Thus, there is an extensive cooperation in the field of economic development for India.

Modi's Maiden Visit to the Himalayan Country

During Modi's two-day visit, both countries put forward their commitment to extensive development cooperation and discussed ways and means for further enhancement of ties. Modi inaugurated India's assisted project, the building of the Supreme Court of Bhutan, and laid the foundation stone of the 600 MW Kholongchu Hydro-electric project.[13] He also announced a number of measures and concessions including the exemption of Bhutan from any ban on export of milk powder, wheat, edible oil, pulses and non-basmati rice. The two sides recalled the free trade arrangement between them and the expanding bilateral trade and its importance in further cementing their friendship. India and Bhutan reiterated their commitment to achieving the 10,000 MW target in hydropower cooperation and not to allow their territories to be used for interests "inimical" to each other. PM Modi also mooted the idea of an annual hill sports festival with India's north-eastern states along with Bhutan and Nepal. He also announced the doubling of scholarships being provided to Bhutanese students in India which worth two crores. He also promised that India will also assist Bhutan set up a digital library which will provide access to Bhutanese youth with two million books and periodicals.

Challenges and Road Ahead

There are issues posing serious challenges to security and integrity of the country. Twenty-three rounds of talk between China and Bhutan have failed to solve 420 km border disputes of Jakarlung valley, Pasamlung valley and Doklam plateau.[14]

The Siliguri Corridor is a vital tri-junction between Bhutan, Bangladesh and Nepal, and there is a narrow hub of rail, road and air arteries just about 30 km wide which is 500 km from the Chumbi Valley. In shocking developments, the Chinese leadership has been issuing statement like "Bhutanese, Sikkimese and Ladakhis form a united family in Tibet.[15] They have always been subject to Tibet and to the great motherland of China. They must once again be united and taught the communist doctrine", which is grave concern not only for Bhutan but India as well. Though diplomatic relations between Bhutan and China have not been established, the capital city's market is already flooded with 'Made in China'—shoes, silk, toys, heaters, and kitchen utensils and 'Hong Kong market'.[16] China is planning to lay an extension line stretching the Tibet railway from Lhasa to the borders of India, Nepal and Bhutan by 2020. On the other hand, Japan is very much interested in developing infrastructure. These developments are a setback to India as they are edging over New Delhi. Furthermore, deepening roots of democracy, climate change and frequently occurring natural calamities are also major hurdles in ensuring sustained relations.

However, as observed by George Modelski, "Foreign policy involves all activates of a nation by which that nation is trying to change the behaviour of other nation and to adjust its own behaviour in the international environment". This definition is applicable in principle as well as practice in the India and Bhutan context as there are many more actors are ready to take risk to exploit the full potential of Thimpu to safeguard their national interests. Thus, the Confederation of Indian Industry (CII) has found out the potential sectors of economic cooperation between India and Bhutan, namely Hydro Power, Agro Processing, Education, Tourism, Horticulture, ICT and ICT-enabled Services and Environment Management. Hence, these are golden opportunities to nurture the natural choice friend and complete the projects without further delay. There is also an urgent need not to go behind the shortsighted policies like withdrawing subsidy of kerosene when the country is at the crossroads. This will open Pandora's Box of problems rather than solving issues. Very importantly, keeping a hawk eye on the Chinese shadow over India and Bhutan bilateral relations and its deliberate attempts like Package Deal and Compromise and Concession formula remain as a big challenge. Territorial disputes should not be solved in the absence of the affecting parties of the region. Enhancing people-to-people contact and cooperation between the two countries will help a lot in curbing insurgency and extremism in the north-eastern part of the country.

Above all, creating job for unemployed youths of 'the thunder land' is a need of the hour as it would check anti-India feelings. This is also an opportunity to India where it can enlarge its market through investment and industry in the areas such as agriculture, pharmaceutical industry and splendid tourism to boost both the economies.

Conclusion

New Delhi and Thimpu have traditionally enjoyed harmonious and friendly relations. In fact, "Bhutanese are more comfortable with India. No one should have any doubts about that. If there has been some contact with China by the Bhutanese, it is merely an assertion of our independence and a desire to maintain cordial relations with all our neighbours, without distinction. Bhutanese are a friendly people – we like to be friends with everybody. We have border issues with China and it is clear in my mind that Bhutan cannot resolve those issues by being antagonistic towards them. The historical, cultural, and economic links between Bhutan and India are so entwined and formidable that it will be near impossible to sever this mutually beneficial relationship. I think both Bhutan and India realize this."[17] However, prudence to retain these centuries-old relations and receive challenges posed by the changing environment is strenuous to India. Modi's visit to Bhutan is an outcome of the confluence of these driving forces which reflect a glorious past and a better tomorrow with pragmatic cooperation.

Thus, "We should avoid the mistakes as we made in Nepal and not take smaller countries for granted or act as their big brother. They are sensitive, even touchy on small things, proud and easily hurt. We must respect their sensibilities, honor their national aspirations and win their trust and confidence. They are subject to many pulls and pressures, stress and strains, internally and cannot bear these along without understanding and respect a friendly neighbor like India", T.N. Kaul in his *Diplomacy in Peace and War*. It is a matter of satisfaction that relations between India and Bhutan are friendly and are developing along right lines. They could become model relations of a big country and a small one. We should make efforts honestly and sincerely towards this and we can depend on the young democratic country to reciprocate our efforts in further strengthening friendly relations. In the words of PM Narendra Modi, "India is associated with the progress and happiness of Bhutan and will continue to do so. The two countries are made for each other. The colour of our passports may vary, but our heritage and values remain the same." Hence, both sides need to further reaffirm the trust and confidence for their mutual strategic and economic interests which will ensure a perpetual peace and friendship between both the countries.

REFERENCES

1. 'PM Narendra Modi arrives in Bhutan; gets a red carpet welcome', *Indian Express*, 2014, http://indianexpress.com/article/india/india-others/pm-modi-embarks-on-his-first-two-day-visit-to-bhutan/ (accessed on 20.07.2016).
2. India-Bhutan Friendship Treaty, http://mea.gov.in/Images/pdf/india-bhutan-treaty-07.pdf (accessed on 20.07.2016).
3. Republic Day: Bhutan King chief guest at 26th Jan parade, 2013, http://articles.economictimes.indiatimes.com/2013-01-26/news/36564065_1_jigme-

khesar-namgyel-wangchuck-republic-day-celebrations-chief-guest (accessed on 20.07.2016).

4. India-Bhutan Relations, http://mea.gov.in/Portal/ForeignRelation/Bhutan-February-2012.pdf (accessed on 20.07.2016).
5. Nehru Wangchuck Scholarship Scheme, http://www.indianembassythimphu.bt/pages.php?id=105 (accessed on 20.07.2016).
6. Bhutan - River Systems - Country Data, www.country-data.com/cgi-bin/query/r-1462.html (accessed on 20.07.2016).
7. Case Story on Cross-border Power Export from Dagachhu Hydropower Development. Green Power Development Project Asian Development Bank, http://www.oecd.org/countries/bhutan/48651659.pdf ADB Project Case study (accessed on 20.07.2016).
8. Ideas at the confluence of Energy, Economy & Environment, http://qedbhutan.com/wp-content/uploads/2015/05/E3_Conference_Proceedings.pdf (accessed on 20.07.2016).
9. Inter-Governmental Agreement between Bhutan and India on development of Joint Venture Hydropower Projects, 2014, http://www.mea.gov.in/press releases.htm?dtl/23230/InterGovernmental+Agreement+ between + Bhutan +and +India+on+ development+of+Joint+Venture+Hydropower+Projects (accessed on 20.07.2016).
10. India-Bhutan Trade Relation, http://www.indianembassythimphu.bt/pages.php?id=42 (accessed on 20.07.2016).
11. Economic Cooperation with Bhutan, http://www.indianembassythimphu.bt/pages.php?id=33 (accessed on 20.07.2016).
12. A Good Neighbour Important for Happiness: PM Narendra Modi Tells Bhutan, http://www.ndtv.com/india-news/a-good-neighbour-important-for-happiness-pm-narendra-modi-tells-bhutan-578417 (accessed on 20.07.2016).
13. Joint Press Statement on the State Visit of Prime Minister of India to the Kingdom of Bhutan, 2015, http://pib.nic.in/newsite/PrintRelease.aspx?relid=105683 (accessed on 20.07.2016).
14. Brian Benedictus, 'Bhutan and the Great Power Tussle', *The Diplomat*, 2014 http://thediplomat.com/2014/08/bhutan-and-the-great-power-tussle/ (accessed on 20.07.2016).
15. Ibid.
16. Bhutan between two Giants Sherpem Sherpa<http://www.worldpolicy.org/journal/winter2013/bhutan-between-two-giants>, [accessed on 20.07.2016]
17. Brian Benedictus, 'Bhutan and the Great Power Tussle', *The Diplomat*, 2014, http://thediplomat.com/2014/08/bhutan-and-the-great-power-tussle/ (accessed on 20.07.2016).

8

Proximity to Connectivity: India's Foreign Policy Course towards Bangladesh

Sreelekha K.R.

India has been sharing a unique relationship with Bangladesh since its inception. The present Bangladesh had been a part of 'the great Bengali civilization' known for its secular and inclusive culture. Bangladesh has a shared history with India until 1947, but was destined to be part of the newly formed state 'United Pakistan' with the Partition of the Indian Subcontinent in the same year. The unhappy relationship between West Pakistan and East Pakistan resulted in a civilian political unrest in the then East Pakistan that was confronted with brutal force of the military, and chaos prevailed thereafter. Finally, India intervened in the domestic crisis of East Pakistan and led its liberation from West Pakistan and a new state was formed in 1971, known as Bangladesh.

When a new government was formed under the leadership of Prime Minister Narendra Modi in May 2014, speculations prevailed over the course the foreign policy would take towards Bangladesh due to the political ideology of the Bharatiya Janata Party and the comments made by Narendra Modi about Bangladeshi illegal immigrants during his election campaigns in West Bengal and Assam. But the picture has changed since his 'oath of office' as Prime Minister of India. Prime Minister Modi signalled a warm preference towards India's neighbours by inviting heads of governments of all South Asian states to attend his 'oath of office' ceremony. By making an impressive start by announcing the 'neighbourhood first' policy, Modi declared his interests to bring prosperity and connectivity in the region.

Speculation surrounding Modi's foreign policy towards Bangladesh ended soon after External Affairs Minister Sushma Swaraj paid the first stand-alone visit to Bangladesh on June 26–27, 2014. Minister Sushma claimed that her visit was 'satisfying' and that it had made an 'excellent beginning'.[1] During her visit to Bangladesh, the External Affairs Minister handed over Prime Minister Narendra Modi's letter to the Bangladeshi Prime Minister, as a token gesture of India's interest to join hands with Bangladesh to bring prosperity and connectivity. In the letter, Modi wrote that, for India, Bangladesh was 'not merely a neighbour, but a nation with which we share history, culture, civilization and enduring links between people'.[2] During the first visit itself the new government was enthusiastic to engage and partner with Bangladesh. New Delhi was keen to use the term 'equal partners' when referring to the future bilateral initiatives of both the states.

Though there is a close cultural similarity and shared history between India and Bangladesh, there are certain contentious issues and challenges to security that are left unattended by both the states, but are cardinal to improve bilateral relationship. Porous border, vague maritime boundary, illegal migration, intrusion of criminals though across the border, human trafficking for bonded labour and flesh market, river water disputes, lack of facility to promote interstate trade and commerce, lack of connectivity both for transport and communication and lack of joint mechanisms to address these crises are hindrances to a cordial relationship between both the states.

A breakthrough happened in the India–Bangladesh bilateral relationship when the Modi government succeeded in identifying the issues which were cardinal to the problem, at an early stage of the bilateral process. The maiden visit paid by India's External Affairs Minister to Bangladesh was remarkable with the swift decision to revive various joint decision-making fora like the Joint Consultative Commission, Coordinated Border Management Plan (CBMP), etc. It is also to be noted that almost all the issues identified in the Joint Consultative Commission have been effectively addressed within two years.

Addressing the Contentious Issues/Talking Business

The External Affairs Minister's first visit to Bangladesh deserves a special mention owing to the fact that the meeting addressed a range of core issues including the easing of the visa regime, security concerns, consensus on trade transit routes, sharing of concerns regarding Teesta water dispute, ratification of Land Boundary Agreement (LBA), etc. The proposed goodwill visit of the External Affairs Minister achieved certain concrete results such as providing multiple-entry visa to children under 18 and people above the age of 65, pledging of ratification of Land Boundary Agreement (both the states reached a consensus to start a new Dhaka-Shillong-Guwahati bus service), plan to open four more border *haats* (markets) in Meghalaya, increasing the frequency of the Moitree Express, selling additional 100 MW electricity from Tripura, and finally to extradite Bangladeshi criminals who had used the porous border to take refuge in India after committing crime in Bangladesh.[3]

The new government succeeded in maintaining the momentum by initiating DG-level talks between the Border Security Force (BSF) and the Border Guard Bangladesh (BGB), held at New Delhi in August 2014, which was followed by the 15th Home Secretary level talks of the Joint Working Group (JWG), held at Dhaka on September 2014; in these fora Bangladesh assured India that its soil will not be allowed to be used for terrorism against any country, particularly India.[4] Stemming energy from these policy initiatives, New Delhi held the third India–Bangladesh Joint Consultative Commission (JCC) on September 2014.

Generally, states tend to avoid contentious issues from their bilateral talks, but in the case of India–Bangladesh bilateral relationship, the new government is maintaining a very proactive policy towards its eastern border neighbour. The Joint Consultative Commission, led by respective Foreign Affairs Ministers of both India and Bangladesh, discussed in detail various issues where immediate action was necessary for a peaceful and progressive bilateral relationship. The Joint Consultative Commission carried forward the enthusiasm expressed by both the states in their march towards a close cooperation. The forum also negotiated a wide range of issues, which were contentious to a bilateral relationship between both the states. Both the states reiterated their commitments towards the settlement of *Feni* and *Teesta* water disputes. In order to address illegal migration from Bangladesh and to check the criminal cases, the forum decided to hold regular meetings of DCs/DMs of clusters of bordering districts, setting up of and upgrading of Land Customs Stations (LCSs)/ Land Ports Integrated Check Posts (ICPs), preparation of the Detailed Project Report (DPR) for the Inland River Port at Ashuganj, and DPR for the Rail Container Depot at Ishwardy as decided in the Inter-Governmental Railway Meeting; the issue of upgrading/strengthening of the Ashuganj–Akhaura road was also discussed. Both ministers agreed that the waterways offer a cost-effective and environment friendly means of transport and emphasised that there is great scope for effective utilisation of the Protocol on Inland Water Transit and Trade (PIWTT). Both the parties also agreed to enhance telecommunication connectivity between the two countries and stressed the need for effective implementation of the Coordinated Border Management Plan (CBMP), including regular coordination and exchanges between nodal officers at different levels for better border management so as to prevent cross-border criminal activities, illegal movement, incidents of violence and tragic loss of lives.[5]

Settlement of Maritime Boundary Dispute between India and Bangladesh

The increasing strategic significance of 'Bay of Bengal' in international relations is one of the major reasons of India's decision for a proactive engagement with this littoral state. The verdict of Permanent Court of Arbitration (PCA)'s settlement on the dispute regarding the delimitation of the maritime boundary between India and Bangladesh awarded Bangladesh 19,467 sq km of the 25,602 sq km sea area of the Bay of Bengal.[6] Bangladesh initiated the arbitration process under Annexure VII of United Nations Convention on the Law of the Sea 1982, requesting the tribunal to identify land boundary terminus of both the states and to delimit each state's territorial sea, exclusive economic zone and continental shelf within and beyond 200 nautical miles, where the claims of both the states overlapped.

The verdict of PCA came in July 2014, after five years of legal procedures. The significance of this verdict is that both the binding parties have accepted the verdict with a democratic spirit. Sayed Akbaruddin, spokesperson, External Affairs Ministry, India, declared that 'we are committed to abiding by the outcome of that process'.[7] Though India has been portrayed as a hegemonic power in the region, its flexibility to approve of this verdict shows India's commitment to the international law and UN. There are instances in world politics when states hesitate to accept the verdict of UN/international laws; the latest in this series is the Chinese rejection of arbitration on maritime dispute regarding the South China Sea, filed by Philippines in 2013 under the United Nations Convention on the Law of the Sea. The verdict is likely to be pronounced in the second week of July 2016. China claims that the court has no jurisdiction and that it wants to solve the issue bilaterally.[8] Hence, India's stance of approving the tribunal's verdict has been praised by many South-East Asian states and symbolises India's strength and commitment with regard to democracy. Reciprocating the warmth of Indian response, Bangladesh's Foreign Minister Abul Hassan Mahmood Ali, after reviewing the tribunal's award, declared that 'it is a victory for both States, it is the victory of friendship and a win-win situation for the peoples of Bangladesh and India because it finally resolves peacefully and according to international law – a problem that had hampered the economic development of both states for more than three decades'.[9]

The significance of mutual acceptance of this verdict is that the move will further facilitate the bilateral relationship in the following areas:

- Political and strategic partnership in Bay of Bengal
- Fostering economic cooperation in the region
- Exploration of oil and natural gas in the Bay region

The Union Government's acceptance of this verdict has been considered as a diplomatic breakthrough for various reasons. The emerging influence of Chinese influence in the Bay region can now be defended with improved strategic alignment with Bangladesh. Due to the maritime dispute between India and Bangladesh, oil exploration companies were withdrawn from the assigned projects; hence, settlement of this issue will clear such hurdles. The Bay region known for its rich stock of hydrocarbons will become a source of income and development for both the states.

New Delhi is keen to revive the moribund Bay of Bengal Initiative for Multi-Sectoral Technical and Economic Cooperation (*BIMSTEC*) under the leadership of India and may deliver more desired results.

'Sea-ward Looking Policy'

Prime Minister Narendra Modi revived India's foreign policy priorities, especially in its South Asian context. Decades-old practice of India's 'inward looking' foreign policy practice has been subject to change under the leadership of Narendra Modi. The old policy has been replaced with a new 'sea-ward looking' practice, which signifies the relevance of the ocean, maritime boundaries of the state, marine wealth and, above all, importance of littoral states of Indian Ocean Region and Bay of Bengal which are pivotal to India's strategic security. The Modi government has identified 'ocean' as an unexplored sphere of activity in the Indian context, but the challenges and opportunities provided by the maritime world are abundant.

India's response to its littoral neighbours invites special attention on the background of aforementioned reasons. Democratic and peaceful settlements of maritime disputes are necessary for a viable strategic partnership with concerned states. India has already settled maritime boundary disputes with Sri Lanka, Myanmar and Thailand; the latest in this series is Bangladesh.

The growing Chinese influence in the Bay region poses challenge to sovereignty and security of India. In order to counter this move, a close cooperation with littoral states of this region may produce desired results.

Modi government's dream projects like 'Mausam' and maritime 'Spice Route' envision to reclaim India's lost glory in trade and transit route along the littoral states of Indian Ocean, Bay region and Arabian Sea. Project 'Mausam' aims to reclaim the ancient maritime trade route and cultural links with the multifaceted Indian Ocean world. 'Spice Route project' is a natural extension of the project 'Mausam'. The Spice Route project envisages linking India by revisiting the ancient sea route with Europe, Africa and Asia.

Both these projects are an ambitious foreign policy initiative of the Modi government, which are primarily designed to defend Chinese 'Belt and Road' projects, which is intruding into India's space.

Land Boundary Agreement (LBA)

The Radcliffe Line became the border demarcation line after the partition of the Indian subcontinent into India and Pakistan in 1947. The same line demarcated India from East Pakistan until 1971 and continued to be the borderline between India and Bangladesh after 1971. Since 1947, there had been a number of attempts made to settle this porous boundary, but in vain, due to the hostilities that prevailed between both the states. India and Bangladesh were able to conclude the Land Boundary Agreement on 1974, after the independence of Bangladesh, to settle the vague boundary demarcation. The unresolved status of this issue created pandemonium in the border area and denied civic amenities to people inhabiting in these areas. In 2010, out of India's and Bangladesh's desire to reach out a final solution to the longstanding problem, detailed negotiations, joint visits to the areas and land surveys were undertaken, which finally led to the signing of a protocol in September 2011. The protocol forms an integral part of the LBA 1974 and is subject to exchange of instruments of ratification by the governments of India and Bangladesh.[10]

Ratification of Land Boundary Agreement was a historic achievement of India–Bangladesh bilateral relationship. The vigour expressed by Prime Minister Narendra Modi to advance with this policy option is a golden feather in his foreign policy endeavour. Premiers of India and Bangladesh finalised the agreement in June 2015, and subsequently the agreement became effective from July 1, 2015. Ratification of the agreement resulted in the demarcation of boundary in all the undemarcated segments, exchange of 111 Indian enclaves in Bangladesh with 51 Bangladesh enclaves in India, and a resolution of all adversely possessed areas.[11]

By ratifying the LBA, the Modi government is in a position to use opportunities presented by Bangladesh with regard to regional cooperation and strategic security. The landmark agreement on LBA provides India an ocean of opportunity; it will help India to settle its porous border areas, cross-bordering of criminals, illicit trade and business, etc. Above all, a clearly demarcated boundary helps the authorities to avoid clashes and to forge a close cooperation. Hence, Modi's audacity to embrace such a policy option justifies his neighbourhood first policy.

Trade and Transit Routes

India's bilateral relationship with Bangladesh has achieved a remarkable zenith under the Modi government. Trade and transit connectivity is a major concern for the Modi government in the South Asian region. Since the inception of his government, Narendra Modi has emphasised an effective utilisation of the Protocol on Inland Water Transit and Trade (PIWTT) in the Bay region. This project materialised on June 19, 2016, with the Kolkata-Ashuganj-Tripura transit facility[12] connecting both land and waterways for regional trade promotion. This transit mode effectively reduced the time and cost of shipments in the Bay region. This transit route also facilitates regional connectivity by allowing Bangladesh to transit goods to Nepal and Bhutan via India, while India can access Myanmar via Bangladesh. On June 15, 2015, BBIN (Bangladesh Bhutan Nepal India) Motor Vehicle Agreement was signed amongst these states, an initiative that was primarily articulated by the leadership of India. The agreement aims to promote passengers, personal and vehicular traffic and to facilitate cross-border movement of passengers and goods. The agreement is expected to 'promote safe, economical efficient and environmentally sound road transport in the sub-region' and will help to create 'an institutional mechanism for regional integration'.[13]

The main objective of this agreement is to increase people-to-people contact and enhance economic cooperation in the region, but this part is missing in the South Asian region when compared with other regional systems. India's foreign policy course, under the stewardship of Prime Minister Narendra Modi, aims to promote sub-regionalism amongst its North-Eastern neighbours in the best possible way, suited to the region and for the maximisation of India's national interest.

Development as a Short Cut to North-East India

India's improved relations with littoral states in the Bay region have literally enhanced the opportunities for North-Eastern states of India. With the signing of BBIN MVA, in June 2015, the region has been connected and exposed legally to Bangladesh, Bhutan and Nepal. Modi government's decision to start the Kolkata-Dhaka-Agartala bus service has brought the people and region together for development and cooperation. Premiers of both the states flagged off a Dhaka-Shillong-Guwahati bus service in October 2015, which has been another milestone with regard to connectivity. The materialisation of Protocol on Inland Water Transit and Trade (PIWTT) in June 2016 was another landmark in connecting this region with the rest of the world. The ambitious Multi-Nation Trans-Asian Railway (TAR) project and Agartala–Akhaura rail link project to connect India with Bangladesh are under process. Fruition of these projects will foster economic and social development of the North-Eastern states and can undo social and economic injustice that the North-Eastern states have faced so far.

Strategic Significance of the 'Bay of Bengal'

India's interest in 'the Bay region' is so significant that it is derived out of various factors which are cardinal to India's national interest, economic prosperity and regional connectivity and security, etc. Possessing a key position in the Bay region may defend the security of India from possible threats from the South-East Asian littoral states. This may also help India to pose a defensive posture towards the 'Pearl of String' strategy adopted by China in the surrounding region. Since, the Bay region is prone to refugee problem, ethnic strife, maritime crimes, etc., holding a major position in this region assures India an opportunity to check these menaces. India's strategic significance will be improved if it can have control over the bay region through which the Sea Lines of Communication are passing through.

India, being a leading military power in the Bay region can act as a 'net security provider' to the region. This reflects India's aspiration to take a leading strategic role in the region and expand its strategic reach even up to the Pacific. India's adherence and commitment to BIMSTEC-like organisations ensures its drive for a collectivity based on security and economic prosperity of the region. Prime Minister Narendra Modi's ever-expanding representations to various bilateral and multilateral fora seem to suggest that empowering India through collective reorganisation of the region may better serve India's interest.

Proximity to Connectivity

India's proximity and connectivity with Bangladesh has gained momentum under the Prime Ministership of Narendra Modi. The political investment made by the Modi government to improve India's relationship with Bangladesh was visible from the initial stage of its development. The Joint Consultative Commission's meeting, immediately within few months of the new government's induction into power, deliberated a detailed list of sectors that have to be addressed to improve bilateral relationships. In fact, the Modi government has won to address and produce concrete results on those identified sectors in the Joint Consultative Committee's consideration. Modi government's motto of 'proximity to connectivity' proved concrete in the following areas:

- Connecting people and the region through land and water
- Connecting people and the region through telecommunication

- Connecting through economic activity, by establishing more border huts along India–Bangladesh border, initiatives under BBIN, etc.
- Improving connectivity through people-to-people contact

Challenges Ahead

Though India achieved phenomenal improvement in bilateral relationship with Bangladesh under the Prime Ministership of Narendra Modi, there are potential challenges that may undermine what it has achieved. Influx of illegal migration is a major issue in the Indo-Bangladesh relationship, as human trafficking both for bonded labour and flesh market poses challenges to economic security and creates health hazards like HIV, and the distribution of arms and ammunitions to separatist movements of India's North-Eastern states creates volatile security issues in India. And above all, increasing Islamic fundamentalist tendencies in Bangladesh create a sturdy situation, in which secular and democratic institutions, organisations and individuals are targeted and face annihilation. Hence, it is time for India and Bangladesh to strengthen their democratic-secular tradition and move forward for a better world.

REFERENCES

1. 'Swaraj's Dhaka trip makes excellent beginning', *The Hindu*, 27 June 2016
2. Habib, Haroon, 'A good start', *The Frontline*, 25 July 2014.
3. Smruti S. Pattanaik, 'Sushma Swaraj's visit to Bangladesh: A new beginning?', 2014 URL: http://www.idsa.in/idsacomments/SushmaSwarajsvisitto Bangladesh_ sspattaniak_300614 (accessed on June 13, 2016).
4. 'Joint Statement on the Third Meeting of the India-Bangladesh Joint Consultative Commission', MEA (2014) URL: http://www.mea.gov.in/bilateraldocuments. htm?dtl/24024/Joint%2BStatement%2Bon%2Bthe%2 BThird%2BMeeting %2Bof%2Bthe%2BIndiaBangladesh%2BJoint%2BConsultative%2BCommission (accessed 13 June 2016).
5. 'Joint Statement on the Third Meeting of the India-Bangladesh Joint Consultative Commission', Ministry of External Affairs, 2016 URL: http://www.mea.gov.in/ bilateraldocuments.htm?dtl/24024/Joint%2BStatement%2Bon% 2Bthe% 2BThird %2BMeeting%2Bof%2Bthe%2BIndiaBangladesh%2BJoint%2BConsultative%2BCommission (accessed 20 June, 2016).
6. Habib, Haroon, 'Bangladesh wins maritime dispute with India', *The Hindu*, 2014, http://www.thehindu.com/news/national/bangladesh-wins-maritime-dispute-with-india/article6191797.ece (20 June 2016).
7. Ibid
8. 'China offers Philippines talks if South China Sea court ignored: China Daily', URL: http://www.reuters.com/article/us-southchinasea-china-philippines-idUSKCN0ZK06E?il=0 (accessed on 4 July, 2016).

9. 'Press statement of the Hon'ble Foreign Minister on the verdict of the Arbitral Tribunal/PCA', Ministry of Foreign Affairs, Government of Bangladesh, 2014, URL: http://www.mofa.gov.bd/media/press-statement-hon%E2%80%99ble-foreign-minister-verdict-arbitral-tribunalpca, (accessed on 17 June 2016).
10. 'India and Bangladesh - Land Boundary Agreement', Ministry of External Affairs, Government of India, p. 11, URL: https://www.mea.gov.in/Uploads/PublicationDocs/24529_LBA_MEA_Booklet_final.pdf (accessed on 3 July 2016).
11. Ibid, p. 4.
12. 'Shipment arrives in Tripura under new India-Bangla transit protocol', *Business Standard*, URL: http://wap.business-standard.com/article/news-ians/shipment-arrives-in-tripura-under-new-india-bangla-transit-protocol-116061900539_1.html (accessed on 24 June 2016).
13. 'Bangladesh, Bhutan, India and Nepal (BBIN) Motor Vehicle Agreement for the Regulation of Passenger, Personal and Cargo Vehicular Traffic amongst BBIN', *Press Information Bureau,, Government of India*, 2015, URL: http://pib.nic.in/newsite/PrintRelease.aspx?relid=122416 (accessed on 24 June 2016).

9

Foreign Policy Prescriptions in the Maritime Neighbourhood of India: Challenges and Opportunities

Commodore R.S. Vasan, IN (Retd)

The importance of being relevant and influential in the only ocean named after a nation—India—apparently was lost on the previous Government. Despite the famous statement of Pandit Jawaharlal Nehru on board INS Mysore in 1958 about the importance of the Indian Ocean, the successive leaders appear to have lost sight of this important factor. The then Prime Minister had grasped the importance of the seas and had this to say, "*I look at India...which in a sense may be said to be in the very lap of an ocean. From time immemorial, the people of India had very intimate connections with the seas. Later on the country became weak. Now that we are free, we cannot afford to be weak at sea...history has shown that whichever power controls the seas has India's seaborne trade at her mercy and in the second, India's very independence itself.*"[1]

The Maritime Environment in the IOR

By all yardsticks, the Indian Ocean Region (IOR) has become a focus point for global maritime initiatives. While USA and other Western powers have always been in the Indian Ocean to further their objectives and protect their interests, it is the entry of a new player China that has changed the equations in this arena. It is not that China is suddenly interested in the Indian Ocean. There are historical factors that indicate that it used the maritime silk routes which connected countries from South and South-East up to East China Sea as recorded by a Chinese Buddhist pilgrim's firsthand account.[2] The silk routes over land are aimed to connect with countries in South-East Asia, South Asia, Africa and Europe. In the context of the Chinese interests in the IOR, the expeditions of the Chinese Admiral Zheng are always quoted. These well-recorded expeditions that brought the Chinese fleet to the shores of countries in the Indian Ocean demonstrated that the Chinese like the Indians did use the oceans for promoting trade and commerce in addition to the people-to-people contact for cultural and social relations. The Chinese fishing nets in Kerala which are being used even today indicate the kind of influence that the Chinese practices had on the local people. So while it was silk that took China to different parts of the world, it was spice and religion that took India to far corners of the world.

Moving forward to the present century of the seas, it is clear that the oceans surrounding India will witness a power play of sorts with many extra-regional players playing out their agenda as they jostle for power and influence using many avenues of trade and engagement. The situation is not very different from the days of the East India Company which came to do business and within a few years, was able to add India as a crowning glory to the British Empire.

Concerned with the rise of China as a military and economic power, and considering China to be a challenger to the Numero Uno position of the USA, the USA has recalibrated its policies in the area now recognised as the Indo Pacific Area. The presence and posturing of these powers in the neighbourhood of India has the potential to alter the maritime power dynamics and strategy.

Energy Security and Geostrategy

Energy needs and dependence continue to shape the policies of growing powers such as India and China. Both the countries are heavily dependent on the sea routes for meeting the import requirements of energy products such as oil, gas and coal. The recent figures indicate that the percentage of imports in respect of both the countries is upwards of 80 per cent. While India, due to its geographic location is not seriously affected in transporting the energy products on both its coast, China has long sea lines to traverse to transport its goods from the African coast to its ports after passing through the Malacca Straits. Identified as the 'Malacca dilemma of China', it is a major factor that has also served as an incentive for China to look at many alternatives. The recent initiatives include the Maritime Silk Road announced in October 2013, the 'One Belt One Road' concept announced last year and the China Pakistan Economic Corridor announced this year (2015) with both strategic and economic connotations for the region. The Bangladesh, China, India, Myanmar (BCIM) corridor is again another initiative that will provide the gateway for China to enter the Bay of Bengal. In the Arabian Sea it is the CPEC that will provide the connectivity and entry to the Arabian Sea through the Gwadar port that will be connected through the China Pakistan Economic Corridor or CPEC. The changing contours of security and stability in the Indian Ocean have come about due to many factors which are discussed in the succeeding paragraphs.

Changing Security Paradigm in the Middle East and North Africa (MENA)

The developments in the Arab countries have the potential of changing the politico-strategic landscape. While there were high expectations from the Arab Spring, it did fizzle out due to various reasons. However, it is the Islamic State of Iraq and Levant (ISIL) that has changed the entire dynamics of the Middle East region. There are complex issues involved and it is very difficult to predict the outcome of this turmoil in the region. USA will continue to be a dominant player in the region and is unlikely to withdraw from the area.

The energy security compulsions demanded that the oil flow from the Middle East was free from interference from both States and also the VNSAs. The Carter Doctrine remained and still is relevant though USA is already an energy-independent nation. However, it is felt that the Carter Doctrine though extensively used in discussions actually referred to a subsequent rationalisation of the US Policy in the Middle East.[3] The discovery of the shale gas has changed the energy criticality of USA and it is expected that with the surplus energy products in USA it will soon be an exporting nation. However, this will not result in any reduction of military maritime presence in the areas of interest in the Middle East. This factor is reinforced by the renewed Maritime Strategy of USA which has indicated that the number of maritime units would be increased in the Middle East. It is obvious that the US will not only continue with its policy in the Middle East but will remain relevant as an important player in the coming decades.

Piracy and Anti Piracy Efforts

The incidences of piracy went up exponentially till the first part of the last decade particularly along the Somali coast. This brought about untold misery to the hapless seafarers who were taken hostage and huge sums demanded as ransoms. It took the collective effort of the navies of the world to bring this to manageable proportions. The measures initiated by the owners of the ship along with IMO stipulations also brought out a change. However, as most of the Source Line of Communications (SLOCS) from east to west and vice versa transit close to India, it also brought the High Risk Area within the EEZ of the India creating problems for fishermen who now also had many ships with armed guards passing through their traditional fishing areas. The other important dimension of the increased piracy attacks off Somalia is the coming together of various navies of the world to protect seafarers and ships which were the victims of a well-organised crime syndicate.

While it appeared to be under control off Somalia, the spate of piracy attacks in the recent months in the Malacca Straits is a matter of grave concern to all the maritime nations which are dependent on the safe passage through such choke points for sustaining and promoting seaborne trade. The statistics brought out by both the Regional Cooperative Agreement against Armed Robbery and Piracy (ReCAAP) and also the Piracy Reporting Centre (Kuala Lumpur) clearly illustrates that while the menace of piracy in the African waters has seen a dip, the incidents in the South-East Asian waters including the Malacca Straits has shown an upward trend. In the past, when faced with a similar situation in the said waters, the Lloyds War Committee had declared the entire area as piracy-prone and a High Risk Area (HRA); the insurance costs had spiralled and it took the joint efforts of Singapore, Malaysia, Indonesia and Thailand to work together to contain the piracy incidents. The efforts included joint/ coordinated patrols, entering the waters of the adjacent country without permission for purposes of hot pursuit, Eyes in the Sky (EiS) which allowed the multinational crew from the concerned countries to be on the aerial platform together to coordinate the activities at sea. It may be worthwhile to have similar mechanisms involving all the stakeholder nations to work through ASEAN to have mechanisms in place for joint and or coordinated operations against pirates. The visits by Modi and also the follow-up by the concerned ministries and the Maritime Security Agencies (Navy and Coast Guard,) would go a long way in enhancing the maritime influence that can be wielded by a maritime India.

Maritime Neighbourhood

India is the only country that has an ocean named after it and rightfully, India expresses concern whenever there is external influence to alter the maritime balance in the IOR. The presence in the IOR of the US-led forces and the Soviet-led forces during the height of the cold war did not stop with mere calls and appeals by the third world countries for keeping the Indian Ocean as a Zone of Peace (ZoP).[4] The UN General Assembly had by a resolution 2832(XXVI) adopted in 1971 declared the Indian Ocean as a Zone of Peace. However, this resolution did find support from other nations but hardly changed the ground situation in which the Extra Regional Powers were very active during the cold war in trying to take positions in the warm waters of the Indian Ocean which provided the second strike capability to the nuclear strategic forces from the sanctuary of the Indian Ocean. The cold war rivalry continued till the breakup of the Soviet Union. The cold war did end but not the presence of the sole superpower of the world which had assumed the role of the supercop. The National Security Advisor of India Ajit Doval surprised everyone during an address[5] delivered by him at Galle, Sri Lanka by suggesting that the Indian Ocean be a ZoP. The analysis is that he wanted to keep China which was showing increased interest in the IOR out of this traditional backyard of India while accepting the inevitable presence of USA and the West that are operating mostly in the western Arabian Sea. However, the ground realities are quite different and it would be worthwhile examining the current status in the Indian Ocean.

China Factor

The role of China in our neighbourhood likewise is a factor that can be ignored at one's own peril. Both the long term and the short term plans for securing our interests in the region will be discussed. There is a lot of emphasis being given to the One Belt One Road which has both the land and sea components of the Silk Road. This master plan conceived by the Chinese Leadership and announced in October 2013 has both the economic and strategic implications for the region. It is a bold and imaginative scheme that would also be supported by the Asia Infrastructure Bank which has more than 56 members including India and Australia.

The map below indicates the routes to be developed over land and also the connectivity that is being provided by linking up of the ports of countries in ASEAN, South Asia and Africa.

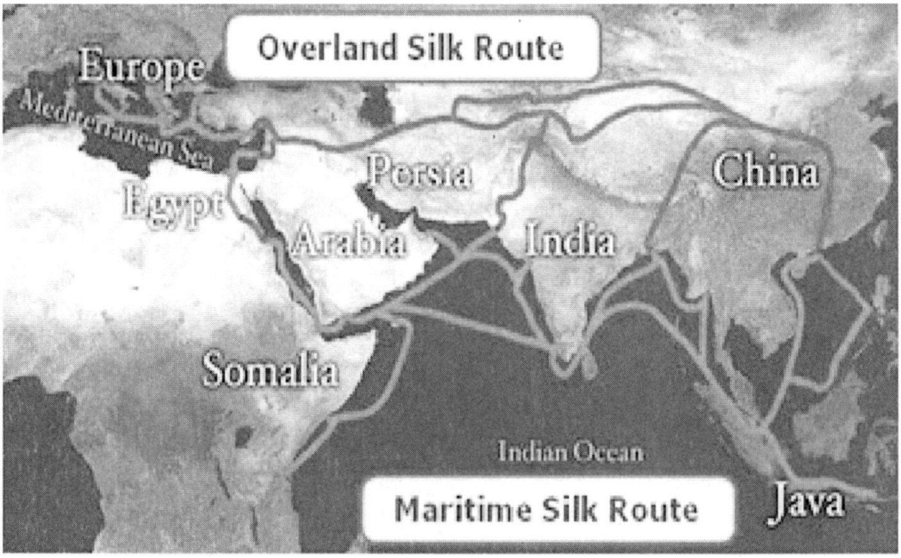

The scale of this ambition is phenomenal as China seeks to use its economic power through the AIIB to help the maritime infrastructure which would help China to also obtain many leverages for the future in the countries where liberal loans and material/technical help is provided to create the necessary infrastructure and ports for enhancing the throughput capacity of ports and harbours which will aid trade and commerce that will immensely benefit China to become the manufacturing hub of the world.

While that is the case on its maritime initiative, over land, by reinventing the silk route over land and investing heavily along the route, China would have a wonderful highway all the way from China to Europe through the Central Asian Republics and Europe. The recent commitment of China to provide up to 46 billion US Dollars for the development of the China Pakistan Economic Corridor would again provide the access to the Arabian Sea by connection through the corridor right up to Gwadar. The fact that the CPEC would also pass through the Pak-Occupied Kashmir despite the protest by India is indicative of the fact that the all-weather friendship with China is paying rich dividends to Pakistan both in strategic and economic terms.

The presence of the PLA Navy units in the Indian Ocean have been a frequent phenomenon particularly since 2008 when the PLA-N units were deployed off Somalia on anti-piracy missions. The presence of the Chinese conventional and nuclear submarines particularly since last year has raised the heckles of the leadership in India.

The factors as highlighted above required careful consideration by the new Government under Modi and there was a felt need to look at the maritime nations near and far to ensure that the strategic interests of India were protected.

Assertive New Stance of Modi's Government

The Prime Minister of India Modi on his part did not waste much time in visiting the countries which are India's maritime neighbours both in the inner circle and the outer circle. These countries by and large remained neglected for decades. The case in example is the visit of an Indian Prime Minister to Sri Lanka after 38 years which came as a fresh whiff of wind to the strained relations between the neighbours and opened up new avenues for cooperation. The initiatives of Modi in the countries around India are covered in the succeeding paragraphs.

Immediate Neighbourhood

The immediate maritime neighbourhood in the definition of this author includes Sri Lanka, Maldives, Myanmar, Bangladesh and Pakistan. Both Bangladesh and Pakistan also share land borders in addition to maritime borders. While India has many other issues with Pakistan both on land and maritime boundary lines, with Bangladesh, plenty of progress has been made when it comes to resolving outstanding issues. The recent Land Border Agreement (LBA) and the award of maritime areas in favour of Bangladesh have added a lot of positivity to the bilateral relations. The visit of PM Narendra Modi to Bangladesh in June 2015, has brought about a whiff of fresh air in the bilateral relations as the two countries exchanged enclaves in which the citizens of the two countries were trapped due to an unimaginative perhaps even intentional legacy from the partition days.

With the proximity of ASEAN countries to Andaman and Nicobar Islands and the historic cultural relations, ASEAN needs to be given special emphasis.

ASEAN Countries

The ASEAN countries are close to the Andaman and Nicobar group of islands than even the mainland of India. With this proximity to the eastern outpost of India which also houses the Tri Services Command,[6] ASEAN has a special place in terms of maritime relations with India. Nurturing good relations with ASEAN countries and also encouraging cooperation in the maritime domain would provide many options for the future. With the growing economic and military clout of China, the ASEAN countries which feel swamped by the Chinese expansionist designs are looking towards India for providing the required strategic and political balance.

As per the MEA annual report 2013-2014, there were engagements with the ASEAN countries and a dialogue was established with Law Enforcement Agencies and other stakeholders on Humanitarian Assistance and Disaster (HADR). There have also been dialogues on maritime security and cyber security with key partners.[7] The airlift of critical relief supplies to the victims of typhoon Haiyan in the Philippines has been lauded and there have been greater exchanges in Science and Technology including in space applications.[8] The biannual event Milan which has been received very well by the participating nations also witnessed the passage exercises with nine warships from South and South-East Asian navies by sailing out together on February 9, 2014[9] after completing various coordination exercises, seminars and table top exercises in Port Blair. Milan[10] as a confidence building interactive programme provides an ideal platform for enhancing the scope of such interaction both with ASEAN and other navies of the region.

The 24th ASEAN summit conducted in Myanmar from May 10–11, 2014 signals the increasing importance being attached to the integration of a democratised Myanmar that would be a link nation in SE Asia. Myanmar will play an important role in the future of ASEAN not just as the Chair but also as a major link both over land and through the surrounding seas.

With the change of Government in India, it appears that there would be additional engagements in the ASEAN which can be identified as the centre of gravity in the newly defined Indo Pacific area. Ms Swaraj, the

Minister of External Affairs of India, has already visited Myanmar, the present Chair of ASEAN in August this year for the East Asia Summit/ ASEAN Regional Forum ministerial meetings. This visit is also important as it is for the first time that India chose to raise the issue of South China Sea by reference to the concept of the freedom of navigation on the highways of the oceans called the Sea Lanes of Communication (SLOCs). It appears that China was embarrassed as it found India joining the chorus of ASEAN members which are very concerned with the aggressive behaviour of China which claims the entire South China Sea.

Close on the heels of this visit came the visit to Vietnam and China indicating the importance attached not only to ASEAN countries but also China which is a key player in the regional security calculus. So the new Government appears quite keen to engage with the ASEAN countries both during formal and informal meetings. While China enjoyed enormous support from Myanmar during the period of its isolation due to the military rulers, it appears that Myanmar on its path to democracy is trying to move away from too much of dependence on China its big neighbour. India has always been interested in Myanmar with historical and cultural relations and now even more so with democracy taking roots.

India which was wary of the military rulers in Myanmar had shunned relations much to its disadvantage. However, India has been actively engaging even with the military junta in Myanmar on the diplomatic, economic and defence fronts over the last several years to counter China's expanding footprint in the Indian Ocean region countries. Myanmar is the only ASEAN country with which India shares land and maritime borders and therefore forms an important link in the security architecture over both land and sea. As recently as on May 8, 2014, India and Myanmar signed a Memorandum of Understanding (MoU) on Border Cooperation.[11] This MoU provides a framework for security cooperation and exchange of information between Indian and Myanmarese security agencies. Apart from providing for coordinated patrols on their respective sides of the international border and the maritime boundary by the armed forces of the two countries, both sides have agreed to exchange information in the fight against insurgency, and the trafficking of arms, drugs, humans and wildlife. Steps to prevent illegal cross-border activities have also been agreed upon.

Two flagship events were organised as part of the commemorative year event to mark the twentieth anniversary of India–ASEAN relations. Firstly, the sailing expedition of INS Sudarshini to ASEAN countries which brought back the memories of the oceanic connectivity in this region that spread the Hindu/Buddhist religion/tradition and cultural practices to the South-East Asian countries. Sudarshini, a naval Sail Training Ship, visited all the ports in South-East Asia to recapture the glory of the Indian kingdoms that wielded considerable influence and built up maritime trade and commerce in the region. Secondly, the ASEAN-India Car Rally, 2012, which brought out the essence of land connectivity which holds great promise for over the land connectivity trade and people-to-people contacts.

Bilateral Exercises

It is clear that the navies of the ASEAN countries are as enthusiastic about conducting bilateral exercises with India which is engaged in building a blue water navy, which is the strongest navy in the Indian Ocean Region. These have contributed immensely in establishing Standard Operating Procedures (SOPs) for inter-operability while working together for facing both conventional and unconventional threats. The details of some of the exercises with the navies of the ASEAN countries are given in the succeeding paragraphs.

SIMBEX (Singapore India Maritime Bilateral Exercise) – The SIMBEX as the name suggests has been conducted regularly enabling the navies to learn from each other. Singapore also has the ReCAAP organisation located where Indian Coast Guard officers are posted regularly to generate and analyse the piracy attacks in the Asian waters. Singapore also has the Data Fusion Center and the International Fusion Center [12] where naval officers from India are deputed to work on data assimilation and sharing in areas of interest. The exercises with Singapore were conducted in the South China Sea from 2005 every alternate year. India has shared its expertise in Anti-Submarine Warfare and other coordination exercises.

Multilateral Exercises

Navies of Singapore, Vietnam, Thailand, Malaysia, Indonesia, Brunei and the Philippines have exercised with India since 1995. This is hosted by the Indian Navy in the Bay of Bengal as the Indo-Thai Coordinated Patrol (Indo-Thai CORPAT) which has been held biannually since September 2005 and is conducted along the maritime boundary line between the two countries. Likewise, the IND-INDO CORPAT (India-Indonesia Coordinated

Patrol) is another bilateral that was started in the year 2000, which is also conducted along the International Maritime Boundary Line (IMBL).

While all the exercises indicated above have ensured that there is Navy-to-Navy dialogue, there are no formailised arrangements with the ASEAN even for Search and Rescue purposes or Humanitarian Aid and Disaster Relief (HADR). What the above demonstrates is that there is active interest on both sides in meeting the challenges in the global commons. However, it may be noted that by and large these have been at the lower spectrum of maritime engagements in the region. The Malacca Straits which is central to the maritime trade and economy in this region is again witnessing an increasing number of piracy attacks. The freedom from pirates which brought in peace and tranquility for a long time is again under threat. There would be a need for the maritime nations of the region to have coordinated efforts similar to those initiated off the Somali coast. The concerted efforts by the navies of the world off the African coast did bring the menace of piracy under control and demonstrated that the collective action by determined navies of the world would ensure the freedom of the seas and safety of transportation along the maritime corridors of the world including through choke points. There is a need to move beyond the bilateral exercises to make the engagements even more meaningful for promoting the regional maritime security and safety architecture. Some of the areas that require attention are illustrated in the succeeding paragraphs.

M-SAR (Maritime Search and Rescue)

While most of the ASEAN nations are signatories to the M-SAR convention[13] despite multinational efforts, there are still many unanswered questions on how MH 370 disappeared evading all forms of surveillance in the region and has still not been found. As per the records, the aircraft flew over Indonesian territory and was well within the radar coverage of the military radars in the region. It was also speculated that the aircraft could have flown over the Andaman and Nicobar Islands during its southwestern journey towards its crash point. Unfortunately, there is nothing definitive about the reasons for the missing aircraft due to not finding the wreckage or the black box even on date. It is here that the ASEAN could take a lead and through the ASEAN Regional Forum (ARF) to work on a model to enhance the surveillance and Search and Rescue architecture keeping in mind the capacity and capability to integrate all the surveillance means available in the region. This hopefully should prevent the kind of situation faced with the disappearance of MH 370.

Illegal Immigration/Human Trafficking

For a long time Indonesia was a hub for facilitating the process of illegal immigration to Australia from its shores. In the recent past, India has also faced the problem of many Sri Lankan Tamil refugees using the shores of India to sail to Australia in unseaworthy boats. India has foiled many such efforts in Tamil Nadu. However, in a recent case, about 157 refugees who left the shores of Puducherry have landed up in detention centres in Australia which has toughened its stand against illegal immigration and human trafficking.[14] The countries of ASEAN and India could work on an arrangement to have preventive measures in place for collective preventive measures to ensure that innocent people are not exploited by the greedy boat owners and syndicates who would make easy money by promising the moon to the poor people who look for greener pastures in Australia, Europe, the US and other developed countries.

Marine Pollution

Though there are International Marine Pollution (MARPOL)[15] statutes, the fragile oceanic areas such as the Andaman Sea are prone to marine pollution due to indiscriminate dumping of marine waste by the ships plying the oceans in these areas. The situation is no different in many parts of the ASEAN seas where human interference and scales of neglect of the environment have resulted in a severe impact on the ecological balance of the seas around many areas. There is a need to engage ASEAN on this score to bring about regional checks and balances to retain the delicate balance of nature. The existing C4ISR arrangements of all nations in the area need to be brought to bear to provide seamless coverage of the areas for prevention of the misuse of the water ways and the oceans for illegal purposes. It could even be a task allocated to the Tri Services Command in Andaman and Nicobar to engage in fruitful discussions during the Milan to put forward implementable recommendations for consideration by the ARF and the SE Asian countries. The setting up of the Tri Services Command[16] has provided multiple options for centralised application of maritime military strategy for furthering the maritime interests of India.

Defence Production

Most of the South East Asian countries are increasing their defence spending and are laying greater emphasis on indigenous production. There have also been constant efforts to obtain technology by offset procedures and transfer of technology options from major arms producers. There also seems to be a desire to be independent of the Chinese influence which in the long run would smother the entire indigenous programme if no efforts are made now. The countries in the region are acutely aware of this aspect that would tilt the balance totally in favour of China which is seen as an adversary when it comes to territorial claims in the South China Sea.

As per the estimates, PRC spent more than 145 bn US Dollars on defence last year (2013). With the conflicting nature of claims particularly in the maritime domain, it appears that there would be no end to even localised armed conflicts. The SE Asian countries therefore would like to move away from the dependence on Chinese products particularly in the defence sector. Some key imports in the region include two submarines for Singapore from France. Vietnam is expected to spend 543 million dollars towards augmenting its maritime capability and surveillance means by buying 32 CG ships. Malaysia is building six ships at a cost of 2.8 billion US dollars with DCNS assistance locally to improve the in-house capability of building warships. Singapore is also a defence exporter since 1971 when it sold defence hardware to Malaysia. With the defence budget of the region expected to reach 40 billion dollars by 2016, there would be opportunities for India to engage with these countries to meet their legitimate demands. It is no secret that these countries are looking at India to balance the influence of China in the region and would like to use the Indian angle as leverage to counter the influence and aggressiveness of China.

While it is acknowledged that India's defence production capabilities are no match for the Chinese capacity and capability, there are key areas in which India has a proven track record. India has succeeded in some of the critical sectors of space and Information Technology. There are also many proven defence products including the Brahmos, Stealthships and other missiles produced under the Integrated Missile Development Programme (IGMDP), a brainchild of scientist Dr A.P.J. Abdul Kalam who retired as the President of India. India is in a position to offer some of these technologies to these countries to help the local industry. The GAGAN programme which is being operationlised for providing regional navigation facility could easily be offered to the SE Asian countries. Likewise, while there is engagement in the IT sector, it needs to be fast tracked to synergise the strengths of the nations in the region depending on the USP of each nation of interest.

Sri Lankan Issues

The closest Island nation Sri Lanka has enjoyed historical, cultural and trade relations. The ethnic struggle and the four *Eelam* wars fought between 1983 and 2009 till the military defeat of the LTTE changed the dynamics of the relations between the two countries. With the defeat of the LTTE a force which was supported by India till the killing of Rajiv Gandhi, Sri Lanka which was facing international scrutiny on its human rights abuses and war crimes started looking increasingly at China for financial and moral support. India had started losing strategic space to China which was looking for footprints in the Indian Ocean Region. The wavering of India and the delays in taking up the offer of building the Hambantota port by India allowed China to become more relevant in various developmental projects including ports and infrastructure. It is only the change of leadership in Sri Lanka that allowed some recalibration of Sri Lanka's policy vis-à-vis China and India. The visit of Modi therefore was both timely and needed to ensure that Sri Lanka remains engaged with India.

Post-2009 scenario, the heavy leaning towards China and India's ambivalence and inaction in Sri Lanka paved the way for China making inroads in every sphere of interest. The heavy investments committed in Sri Lanka were with a view to obtain leverages for the future and also to cement a relation based totally on politico-economic relations. The fact that China did not hesitate to bail out Sri Lanka under the Mahinda regime during the UNHRC meetings meant that Sri Lanka would increasingly bank up on China for such gestures in return for a greater playing field in Sri Lanka. The investments post-2009 were not just in the port sector though the Hambantota and Colombo ports are sited. The investments were in the energy sector, rails and road network and other infrastructure.

Change of Government and Breather for India

With the defeat of Mahinda in the Presidential elections mainly due to the resentment of the Sri Lankan public with the style of functioning and also the charges of large scale corruption, Maithripala Sirisena who was part of the Mahinda Government was elected as the President. Mahinda openly accused the west and also the R&AW for his defeat. The new President demonstrated sensitivity to the concerns of India and showed that he valued the friendship of India.

There has been a purposeful engagement as opposed to the estrangement of the Southern Neighbour by redrawing the contours of Economic, Political, Cultural and Strategic dimensions of relations.

However, the issue of Fisheries, Livelihood and Security has not met much success in terms of resolution as the Tamil fishermen from India and Sri Lanka continue to clash over dwindling fisheries resources in the Palk Bay. This is one sensitive issue that has to be resolved with the active support of the State Government, NGOs and other stakeholders.

The trilateral maritime agreement with Sri Lanka, Maldives and India presents a wonderful opportunity for ensuring that there is greater cooperation amongst the three maritime nations to tackle issues of fisheries, security, environmental concerns, piracy, marine pollution, etc.

The line of credit of $318 million to upgrade Sri Lanka's railways, and the promise to build Trincomalee as a "petroleum hub", and seeking movement on the 500 MW Sampur power project, that has been delayed for years due to environmental concerns are steps in the right direction to ensure that India and Sri Lanka relations scale new heights.

Maldives

This nation has been friendly with India since independence and India has enjoyed great relations both under Gayoom and also under Nashid after his election in a democratic process. However, the recent developments in Maldives have not been favourable to India and there has been some strain in the relations. China also is playing its cards in this country and has made heavy investments. The increased tourist numbers from China has added to the income from that segment. China has also provided plenty of soft loans for adding to the infrastructure. Under the shadow of China–Maldives relations, there is an enhanced need to increase engagement with Maldives, rebuilding the bridges. The traditional relations of decades are in danger of being challenged under the present regime. The eviction of GMR from an important contract for the airport has dampened the spirit of industrialists in India who were till recently the preferred ones.

Though the trilateral agreement is active, there is a need to revitalise this by enhancing the scope of this agreement. Modi, though planned to visit Maldives, could not do so due to the local developments.

There are positive developments both with Bangladesh and Myanmar due to the recent visits and activities that have given new lease of life to the relations between the maritime neighbours.

Extended Neighbourhood

Again, the extended maritime neighbourhood could be considered to include countries as far as Australia and those on the coast of East Africa. The two countries that stand out here are Mauritius and Seychelles which stand out with considerable influence of India due to historic movement of indented labour and traders from India who now form a significant population in these two small maritime countries. The path-breaking initiatives in these two countries on the outer periphery are covered in the succeeding paragraphs.

Mauritius

Prime Minister Modi who is active on the social media tweeted[17] prior to his visit saying *"This week I would be travelling to Seychelles, Mauritius & Sri Lanka. Am looking forward to enhancing our ties with these friendly Nations"*.

The range of Memorandum of Understandings (MoUs) signed is indicative of the rich maritime content with plenty of focus on developing the blue economy. The MoU between India and the Republic of Mauritius was in the field of Ocean Economy, marine resources, fisheries, green tourism, research and development[18] of ocean technology, exchange of experts and other related activities.

There is also an MoU for promoting a Programme for Cultural Cooperation between the Republic of India and the Republic of Mauritius for the years 2015–18. This envisages exchange of cultural troupes, training in fine arts, organisation of cultural exhibitions, preservation of cultural heritage, promotion of Indian languages, exchange of students, etc. This will also enhance greater people-to-people participation between the two countries.

The MoU signed between the Department of Agriculture and Cooperation, Ministry of Agriculture of Republic of India and the Ministry of Agro-Industry and Food Security of Republic of Mauritius for the importation of fresh mango from India will contribute to increasing the volume of trade.

This statement *"I consider our security cooperation to be a cornerstone of our strategic partnership. We intend to quickly build the petroleum storage and bunkering facility in Mauritius,"* has the potential of creating facilities at the outer periphery in a friendly country with significant leanings towards India and provide the necessary leverages as and when so needed.

With the tweet vide PM@narendramodi *"Our agreement on cooperation in Ocean Economy is an important step in deepening our scientific and economic partnership, the stage has been set for enhanced engagement of Mauritius to derive long term benefits."*

While the development of Agalega Island has been on the cards for nearly a decade it is only now that the project seems to get the attention that is due with the statement after signing the agreement about developing the Island *"Our agreement today on the development of Agalega Island is a major stride in our cooperation in infrastructure sector"*.

The bonhomie and reciprocity of sentiments were on display with the statement of the President who said *"I appreciate that Prime Minister Modi and his government has agreed to redirect the Indian line of credit of $ 200 million initially meant for the light railway transit system to projects in the water and energy sector"*.

It is clear that with the visit of the Prime Minister to Mauritius, India has emerged as a preferential partner in developing Mauritius's capability to serve mutual interests. From the point of view of India, it is clear that India is cashing on its traditional links and in the process also ensuring that China does not get a foothold in Mauritius.

Seychelles

The scene was no different in Seychelles, another maritime country with strong Indian connections. A line of credit of 500 mn USD was extended and Barracuda, a fine ship built by the Goa Ship Yard Limited, for Seychelles was commissioned at a ceremony attended by both the leaders. India has an ambitious programme for ensuring that the Maritime Domain Awareness (MDA) is enhanced by synergising the C4ISR efforts of all the maritime nations in the area. The unveiling of the Plaque and Operationalisation of Radar for the CSRS India-Seychelles Cooperation Project paves the way for the realisation of MDA in the areas of interest.

Way Ahead

It is important that India has to ensure that it does not lose sight of the

Strategic Primacy of India in the ocean named after it – The Indian Ocean. While it is claimed that both India and China have enough space for growth, it is clear that the Chinese initiatives in the maritime neighbourhood of India have the potential to destabilise the status quo in the Indian Ocean.

Consistent with the initiatives of PM Modi, it is important to ensure that the inner and the outer lines of maritime periphery of interest are not breached by Extra Regional Players including China. This requires proactive policies and compliance with the provisions of various agreements signed during the visit of Prime Minister Modi.

India has to raise the bar and use all means to raise the levels of engagement in all maritime spheres in our neighbourhood in South Asia, South-East Asia, countries from Africa to Australia, Pacific powers, etc. These need to be leveraged on the benefits of Connectivity, Cooperation, Engagement, Investment, and Aid, Training and soft power application. This would translate to providing options for the future in IOR without conceding space to Extra Regional Players.

It is also important to reexamine the relevance of the prescriptions of one of the greatest strategists of ancient India, Chanakya. Foreign policy prescriptions of the *Arthashastra* have not outlived their utility. There may be a need for minor modifications depending on the present day needs. It is for India under the new Government to revisit the past and move forward to ensure that those days of glory are restored in a new world order. The climate is conducive for such a thrust due to the dynamics of the region which favour India more than China.

REFERENCES

1. Roy, Mihir, *War in the Indian Ocean*, New Delhi: Lancer Publishers, 1995, p. iv.
2. Kauz, Ralph, *Aspects of the Maritime Silk Road: From the Persian Gulf to the East China Sea*, Germany: Harasowitz Gm BH & Co, 2010, p. 156.
3. Meiertöns, Heiko, *The Doctrines of US Security Policy: An Evaluation under International Law*, New York: Cambridge University Press, 2010, p. 154.
4. Subramanyam K, *Self Reliance and National Resilience*, New Delhi: Abhinav Publications, 1975, p. 86.
5. Doval, Ajith, an address made at *The Galle Dialogue* held in Sri Lanka in December 2014.
6. Rajiv, Sikri, *Challenges and Strategy, Rethinking India's Foreign Policy*, New Delhi: Sage Publications, 2009, pp. 252.

7. MEA (2014), Annual Report of MEA 2013-14 URL: http://mea.gov.in/Uploads/PublicationDocs/23873_EXTERNAL_AFFAIR__Eng__AR_2013-14.pdf (accessed on March 10, 2015).
8. Ibid, pp. v, xii.
9. Indian Navy, Government of India, Details available on the navy website *vide,* URL: http://www.indiannavy.nic.in/milan/milan-14-to-culminate-with-passage-exercise.html (accessed on March 6, 2015).
10. Osius, Ted and C Raja Mohan (2013), *Enhancing India ASEAN Connectivity,* Washington: CSIS publication, p.16.
11. India and Myanmar sign Memorandum of Understanding on Border Cooperation, Ministry of External Affairs, Government of India 2014, URL: http://www.mea.gov.in/pressreleases.htm?dtl/23315/India+and+Myanmar+ sign + Memorandum +of+Understanding+on+Border+Cooperation (accessed on February 27, 2015)
12. Jasper, Scoot, *Securing Freedom in the Global Commons,* California: Stanford University Press, 2010, p. 75.
13. International Convention on Maritime Search and Rescue (SAR), International Maritime Organization, URL: http://www.imo.org/About/Conventions/ListOfConventions/Pages/International-Convention-on-Maritime-Search-and-Rescue-(SAR).aspx (accessed on February 27, 2015).
14. Prasad, Srinivas R, 'Australia to act tough with illegal immigrants', *The Hindu,* 2014, URL: http://www.thehindu.com/news/cities/puducherry/australia-to-act-tough-with-illegal-immigrants/article6274812.ece.
15. International Convention for the Prevention of Pollution from Ships (MARPOL), International Maritime Organisation, URL: http://www.imo.org/About/Conventions/ListOfConventions/Pages/International-Convention-for-the-Prevention-of-Pollution-from-Ships-(MARPOL).aspx
16. Ibid
17. Narendra Modi, Twitter Account, 6:53 PM, 8 March 2015 from his tweet as obtained from twitter account of the Prime Minister.

10

India–Sri Lanka Relations: New Hopes on the Horizon

M. Venkataraman

Introduction

The special bond that India has developed with its southern and close maritime neighbour Sri Lanka defines the bilateral political, economic and strategic relations and determines the contours of future relations between the two countries of South Asia. The shared commonalities in terms of ethnicity, language and religion are not only historic but also important factors worth mentioning and have taken their bilateral relations to new heights as well as contributed to irritancy. These have been widely commented and analysed by scholars and it is generally agreed that their relationship has seen both extremes. Sri Lanka has always been considered as India's near abroad and India, in view of its close affinity, has always been influential in Sri Lankan domestic affairs. And India's assertion of influence in Sri Lanka has always been met with opposition and fear from among the majority Sinhala nationality which to a large extent defines the government's domestic and foreign policy. Owing to this Sri Lanka has always attempted to chart its own path and not succumb to the pressures of India. Hence an assertive foreign policy stance could be seen on the part of Sri Lanka to manouvre with a certain degree of freedom given its victory over the liberation struggle waged by the LTTE and the increasing antipathy shown by New Delhi on bilateral issues constrained by regional power politics. However, recent trends in bilateral relations show some progress on the positive side particularly since the assumption of power by Prime Minister Narendra Modi in India and the change of government in Sri Lanka under Maithripala Sirisena. There have been series of high level visits including that of the Indian Prime Minister and reciprocated by the incumbent government in Sri Lanka and several other agreements of importance were signed. All this shows that the past irritant issues have now been sidelined to the better. This paper argues that the bilateral relationship has shown drastic improvements particularly with the change of regime on both sides signalling the 'political will' exhibited by the leadership to improve relations. This paper aims at analysing the recent trend and brings out the factors that have contributed for the same. Accordingly, a brief discussion on the history, political and economic ties in terms of the various pressing issues such as the Tamil question, fishermen problem, dispute over Kacchativu and role of extra-regional powers such as China are in order.

Historical Relations

As far as history is concerned one cannot forget the close religious and cultural ties between India and Sri Lanka. With a recorded history of about 2,500 years Sri Lanka was influenced by the introduction of Buddhism from North India by about 250 BC,[1] which became Sri Lanka's national religion from then on. The importance of this can be seen from the visit paid by the Indian Prime Minister Narendra Modi as recently as in March 2015 to Anuradhapura, which happens to be the cultural capital of Sri Lanka and where for the first time Mahinda, the son of Ashoka the Great, arrived to spread Buddhism. It is symbolic of the Indian cultural and religious ties with Sri Lanka and Prime Minister Modi chose not to ignore this important historical ties that have existed between the two countries. Notably, since then, north India has been a religious destination for several Buddhist monks for centuries and India donated a Buddha statue modelled on the one in Sarnath to Sri Lanka.[2] Sathiya Moorthy (2012)[3] says that the Kapilavastu relics that were brought from India to Sri Lanka for respects to be paid by the Buddhists across the country underlies the long and continuing cultural and religious relations that have existed between India and Sri Lanka. In fact, it has been reported that Gandhiji referred to Ceylon as India's "daughter state" (S. Muthiah, 2003). The other significant historical ties that should be mentioned is the presence of ethnic Tamils—both Sri Lankan and Plantation Tamils—which have tied up the southern

Indian state of Tamil Nadu, which happens to be a contiguous state to Sri Lanka. The Indian Tamils who also form a significant population in Sri Lanka today were brought to Sri Lanka from Tamil Nadu by the British during their colonial rule as plantation workers in 19th century and have their continued religious ties with Tamil Nadu. Most of them have returned while the rest have domiciled in Sri Lanka under the Srimavo–Shastri pact. As also the Sri Lankan Tamils who have lived much before the onset of colonial rule do also acknowledge their Indian ancestry in rural villages in Tamil Nadu along with other religious groups such as the Muslims and Christians. Hence there are two facets of India—one from North India in the form of Buddhism and the other from South India in the form of linkages between Tamils in Tamil Nadu and the Tamils in Sri Lanka. It is these two aspects that continue to be a defining factor in the India–Sri Lanka relations despite all odds.

Political Relations

Sketching the political relationship between India and Sri Lanka is an interesting endeavour not from the point of view of the bloody civil war but from the dimension of how the whole events transpired drawing the attention of distant and immediate neighbours alike. A determining factor in the bilateral relationship is the manner in which the different governments in New Delhi and Sri Lanka approached the various aspects of relationship, be it the Sri Lankan civil war or the issue of fishermen or even the issue of maritime security. Generally speaking, in contrast to the positive tone of the historical relations, the bilateral political relations have not been very cordial and have been marred by mutual suspicion and animosity perceiving each other as a suspect and a threat to the national integrity and sovereignty. Of course, the threats that each other perceive is not in any traditional sense. Rather it is the differing perceptions of how these two nations that led to viewing each other as a "threat" not to the territorial integrity directly but as a threat to their sovereignty. Accordingly, approaches to such perceived threats by the respective governments in New Delhi and in Sri Lanka have led to different outcomes in bilateral relations.

The Problem So Far

The unfolding domestic ethnic politics in Sri Lanka influenced the nature of bilateral political relations between the two countries for a long time.

As noted above, the presence of ethnic Tamils in Sri Lanka predominantly in the Northern and the Eastern provinces of the country was not only geographically connected to the other country but also defined the very nature of their bilateral political ties. The Official Language Act or what is popularly called the "Sinhala only" act of 1956 sealed the division between the Sinhala ruling elites and the Sri Lankan Tamils, who as a result were subsequently marginalised both economically and politically. Since the onset of the Sri Lankan Tamil problem, where the Sinhala majority government ignored the legitimate political aspirations of the ethnic Tamils, India could not disentangle itself from the issue and had to relent to the Tamil sentiments in the southern Indian state of Tamil Nadu. It is well known that the long deprivation of political and economic rights of the Tamils and continued subjugation by the Sinhala majority government neglecting the genuine linguistic and economic rights led to serious consequences. The proposal to devolve political powers to the Northern and Eastern provinces in Sri Lanka was also neglected, which became a vexed issue thereafter. The rise of the liberation movements particularly the Liberation Tigers of Tamil Eelam (LTTE) taking up armed struggle to realise their aspirations were a product of such internal political squabble in which the ruling Sinhala political elites failed to manage properly leading to subsequent involvement and interference by India. Not only that the civil war, popularly called the Eelam war (in four different phases) drew extra-regional powers such as China to intervene by way of supplying military hardware to the Sri Lankan government forces to fight against the LTTE.

Be that as it may, what is important to note is the fall-out on bilateral political relations. India's involvement in the ethnic issue of Sri Lanka can be discussed under two heads: Firstly, the plight of Tamils in Sri Lanka became intertwined with that of the Tamil sentiments in India's southern state of Tamil Nadu and consequently was politicised by Tamil regional political parties (read Dravidian Parties) in Tamil Nadu, which could not be ignored by New Delhi at least during the initial years. Coupled with this was the issue of Tamil fishermen who were deprived of their rights to fish freely that became a frequent cause of worry to both countries. And secondly, the fear on the part of India not to allow the Sri Lankan ethnic problem to become internationalised thereby providing room for its northern neighbours—Pakistan and China—to play a role in it. As regards the Tamil issue, at the height of the Tamil armed struggle in the 1980s regional political parties in Tamil Nadu became increasingly sensitive to the plight of their Tamil brethrens and politicised the issue at the national level asking for intervention and demanding New Delhi to pressurise the Sri Lankan government to devolve powers to the North-Eastern Province where the majority of Sri Lankan Tamils lived. In fact, it has been widely reported that New Delhi and the Tamil Nadu government did extend support to the Tamil militants allowing sanctuary and bases in Tamil Nadu to operate from where they could continue their armed struggle - an issue that became thorny in their bilateral relations in the subsequent years. However, as will be seen later, with the change of government in New Delhi under Prime Minister Narendra Modi the emphasis has shifted to bilateral relations rather than succumbing to the sentiments of regional parties.

One has to note that in this entire episode, India's outlook of Sri Lanka's ethnic problem cannot be seen independent of its larger relationship with Pakistan and China both of which are antagonistic to India's aspirations and have had a history of inimical relations. Hence India fears Sri Lanka's attempt to take military and economic help from these two countries. India was successful in evading Pakistan's role in Sri Lanka but it has not been the case with China.

The signing of the Indo-Sri Lankan Peace Accord in 1987 and the sending of the Indian Peace Keeping Force (IPKF) to disarm the Liberation Tigers of Tamil Eelam (LTTE) was the outcome of such perceptions, which rather than contributing to better relations only deteriorated their bilateral relationship. This is because the agreement was a product of diplomatic pressure exerted upon Sri Lanka by India in order to keep the ethnic issue within the ambit of Sri Lanka and India, which has always been sensitive to any extra-regional presence. As Fr Tissa Balasuriya (1988, p.1038) notes "there is a deep-seated fear of Indian hegemony and Indian expansionism and the statement of Indian political leaders are taken with a pinch of salt given past denials of militant bases and the actions of Indian and Tamil Nadu governments". Besides, the Sri Lankan ruling class looked at the agreement and the presence of IPKF as a threat – a perception that was anticipated too well by the then Sri Lankan political leadership under President Jayawardene.[4] Subsequently, New Delhi was forced to withdraw the IPKF in 1990 without accomplishing much in terms of disarming the LTTE.

The defeat of the LTTE in 2009 did not turn the tide favourably either. The promise to devolve powers to Tamil provinces and resettle the thousands of war-affected Tamil people[5] has not been met with by the Sri Lankan government inviting intense opposition from among the regional political parties in Tamil Nadu.[6] In fact the parties were competing with each other in opposing the actions of the Sri Lankan government and went to the extent of passing a resolution in the Tamil Nadu Assembly demanding referendum to be held in the North-Eastern Province of Sri Lanka and pressurising New Delhi to impose economic sanctions against the country.[7] There were several other protests waged by the political parties apart from attacking Sri Lankan tourists and sending back sports teams besides successfully preventing the Indian Prime Minister from attending the Commonwealth Heads of Government Meet (CHOGM) in Colombo in 2013. The deplorable living conditions and lack of effective measures by the Sri Lankan government led to increasing international pressure in the form of initiating an investigation by the UN Human Rights Council on the alleged human rights abuses committed against the Tamils by the Sri Lankan military during the last phase of the Eelam war.

The approach of the Central government in New Delhi on the matter was quite anticipated. Not only did it succumb to the pressure from the regional political parties but also voted in favour of the UN resolution[8] twice in 2012 and 2013 dealing a new blow to the bilateral relationship as the Sri Lankan government opposed any such international investigation terming the UNHRC resolution as "international conspiracy against the regime, threat to its sovereignty, and plot to punish the government for 'eradicating' terrorism".[9] India's decision to abstain from voting in the newly introduced US-sponsored resolution in 2014 neither contributed to any change of attitude on the part of Sri Lanka. However, it should be noted that India, along with other countries and multilateral institutions, did extend aid for post-War reconstruction efforts such as construction of railway lines, supply of agricultural tools, transport buses for schools and hospitals, supply of tractors and cements for reconstruction, extending financial grant of 9.9 million USD for education and health sectors, etc.[10]

Another irritant issue in the relationship is over the right of fishermen of both countries to fish freely along the Palk Bay region. This has long affected the bilateral relations particularly when fishermen from Tamil Nadu were shot at and arrested raising deep concerns and protests from among the political parties in Tamil Nadu. Despite the signing of maritime boundary agreement way back in 1974 and a supplementary agreement in 1976 agreeing to the delineation of maritime boundary in the Gulf of Mannar in the Palk Bay straits, fishermen from Tamil Nadu were accused of crossing the border leading to arrest and killing by the Sri Lankan Navy. Political parties in Tamil Nadu including the ruling AIADMK government are of the view that the retaking of Kachchativu would only solve the fishermen problem. The gravity of the situation can be noted from the statement made by the Sri Lankan Prime Minister Ranil Wickremasinghe who said that the Indian fishermen may be shot if they intruded in Sri Lankan waters[11] justifying that the shooting does not amount to human rights violations. The Prime Minister further accused India of following double standards citing the case of Italian marines. To quote him:

> This is our waters. Fishermen of Jaffna should be allowed to fish. We stopped them from fishing. That's why the Indian fishermen came in. They (Jaffna fishermen) are willing to have a deal. Let's have a reasonable settlement but not at the cost of the livelihood of northern fishermen.[12]

The issue was taken up during the recent visit by the Indian Prime Minister Narendra Modi to Sri Lanka insisting that both countries should find a long-term solution to the problem as it involves the livelihood of both countries' fishermen.[13] However, incidents of arresting[14] and shooting continue to hamper cordiality and act as irritant factor in bilateral relations.

Some Recent Trends in Bilateral Relations

The change in political leadership in Sri Lanka with Maithripala Sirisena taking over power from the Rajapaksa regime in January 2015 has heralded a new turn in the bilateral relationship towards the positive side. Within a month of taking over as President, Maithripala Sirisena chose to visit India in February 2015 as his first foreign State visit; during his visit several important bilateral agreements were signed. His election manifesto mentioned that he would have closer relations with India that will not be anti-Indian.[15] The visit indeed help strengthen the existing relationship as it saw appreciation from all quarters particularly at a time when India was wary of China's influence in Sri Lanka during the previous government under Rajapaksa. In the words of the President of India:

> The symbiotic relationship between India and Sri Lanka is not based merely on geography, which is compelling enough, but is also

> predicated on shared religions, cultural practices, family ties, linguistic commonalities, economic cooperation, political understanding, and much more. Not many would know that a Sri Lanka student of Gurudev Rabindranath Tagore, Ananda Samarakoon, composed the Sri Lankan national anthem, "Sri Lanka Matha".[16]

Of the several agreements that were signed during the visit, the one on cooperation on the peaceful uses of nuclear energy to build Sri Lanka's nuclear energy infrastructure and also to sell small-scale nuclear reactors for peaceful purposes was a landmark event. Besides, the cultural cooperation agreement and the establishment of Nalanda University were among others that were signed between the two countries.[17] In fact, India did work well to push for these important agreements given the anxiety and concern over China's increasing influence in the country.

Coupled with this was the various initiatives taken by Prime Minister Narendra Modi to prioritise Indo-Sri Lankan relations that were symbolised by his invitation to the then Sri Lankan President Rajapaksa to the swearing-in ceremony at New Delhi. Another signifying act was the visit by an Indian Prime Minister to Sri Lanka in 28 years during which several initiatives were taken to strengthen cordial relations. Among others, Prime Minister Modi asserted that India will take active participation in developing Sri Lanka's economy emphasising the need to deepen and broaden trade ties to address imbalances in bilateral trade.[18] The need to push for a comprehensive economic partnership was also mooted in order that besides trade, goods, services and investments would also be promoted between the two countries.[19] In fact, Prime Minister Modi is said to have stated that his visit was part of his objective of maintaining frequent contact with neighbouring countries.[20] Most importantly, as mentioned above, Modi visited Anuradhapura and Mahabodhi society in Colombo, the two most important places that symbolise the cultural connection between India and Sri Lanka and as an act of public diplomacy. Yet another landmark initiative was his visit to Jaffna, a politically sensitive place for Tamils in both countries besides of course starting off several infrastructural projects such as the flagging off the Indian-sponsored railway line between Talaimannar and Colombo; the two countries also signed agreements on visa, customs and youth development. In the military realm, in contrast to China, India was successful in strengthening its naval ties with Sri Lanka considerably by way of "bilateral exercises, staff talks, training, equipment, senior official visits",[21] etc.

Besides the above, India's deepening of ties can be seen from the support it has extended to develop infrastructural projects mostly in the north of the country such as power plant construction, building of 27,000 new homes and hospital for the war-affected Tamil populace, the dredging of the Kankesanthurai port and the re-construction of the Northern Railway line.[22] These show deepening of ties of between both the states and as a result of successful diplomacy of India to bring Sri Lanka into its trust fold.

Current Level of Bilateral Economic Ties

Notwithstanding the ups and downs in political relations, bilateral economic ties have been slow and steady, particularly in the wake of change of governments on both sides (see figure 1.0). Initially for Sri Lanka it was the Western world that was the target of exports but since the late 1990s and with the signing of the FTA there has been a surge in bilateral trade. This can be seen from the fact that India is the top importer of the island nation (see table 1.0 below) and the third largest export partner as well (see table 1.1 below). An impetus to this trend has been the 1998 India-Sri Lanka Free Trade Agreement (FTA) which came into force in 2000. In fact, the FTA was the first of its kind that India signed with any other country with bilateral trade in 2013–2014 touching $ 5.2 billion with Indian exports amounting to $ 4 billion and Sri Lankan exports to $678 million.[23] According to Saman Kelegama (2014, pp.3-4), the FTA facilitated trade ties between the two countries dramatically lifting up India to be the third largest export partner from the fourteenth position. And since then, the range of commodities exported and imported to Sri Lanka have varied such as electrical machinery and parts, cereals, sugar and confectionery, pharmaceutical products, iron and steel, cotton, vehicles, mineral fuels, mineral oils and nuclear reactors and boilers etc. Table 1.2 below highlights the major imports from India. Some of the exports from Sri Lanka to India were pepper, waste and scrap steel, areca nuts, dried fruit, cloves, and waste paper, insulated wires and cables, animal feed, refrigerators, pneumatic tires, ceramics, vegetable fats and oils, refined copper products, and furniture. The top five imports to Sri Lanka from India include gas oil and diesel, white cane sugar, petrol, motor cycles, and autorickshaws.[24]

Fig. 1.0: Bilateral Trade as of 2013

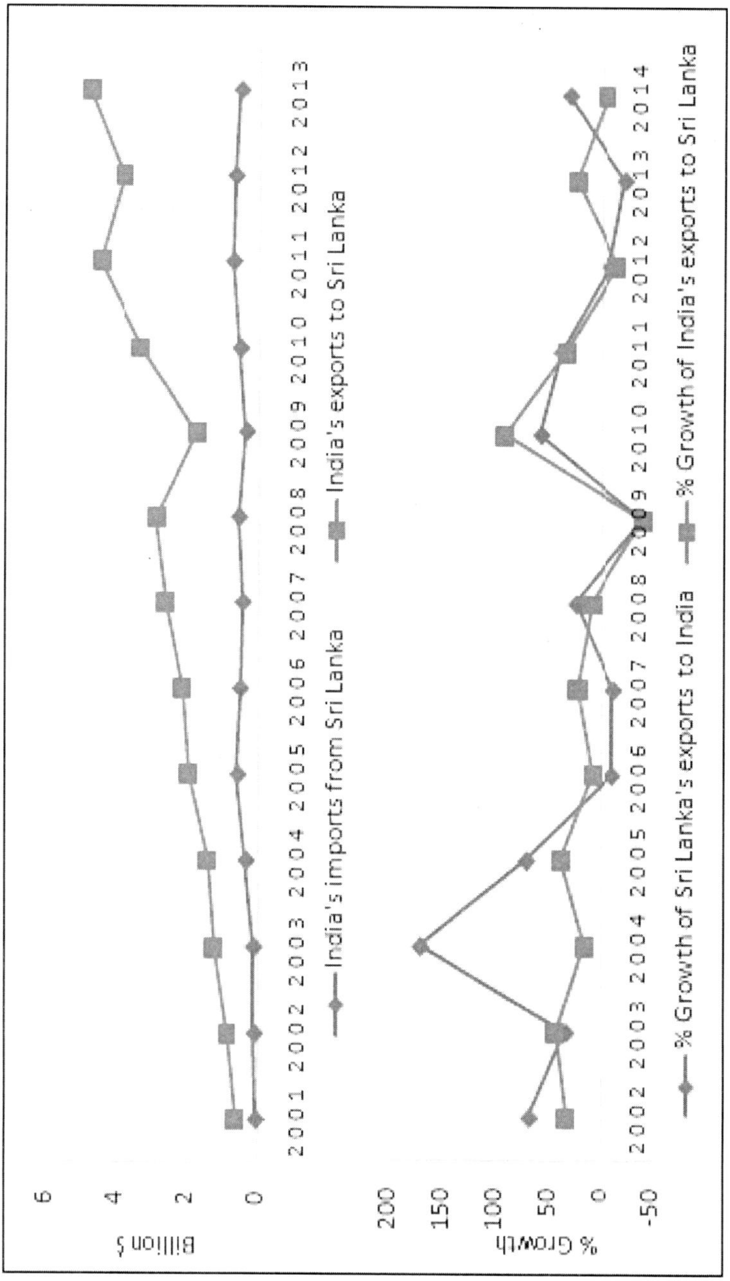

Source: International Trade Center, 2014

India Sri Lanka Bilateral Trade

Table 1.0

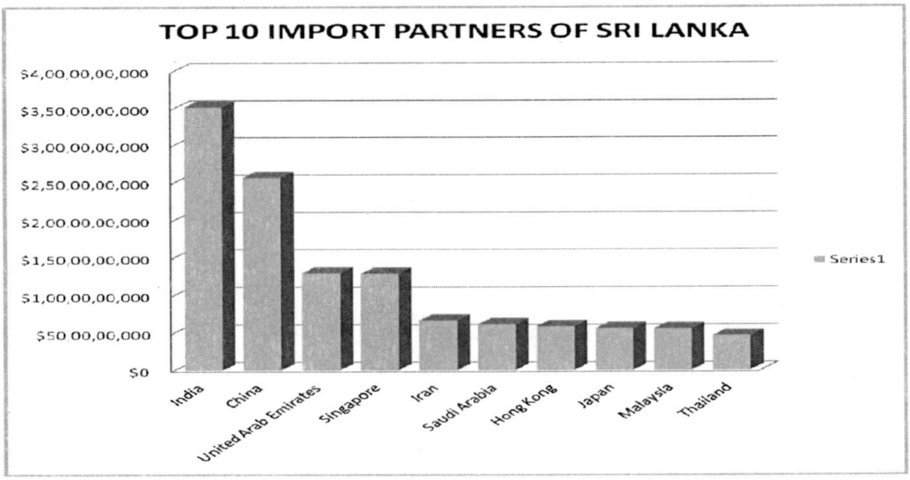

**Source*: Global Edge, Michigan State University (2012).

Table 1.1

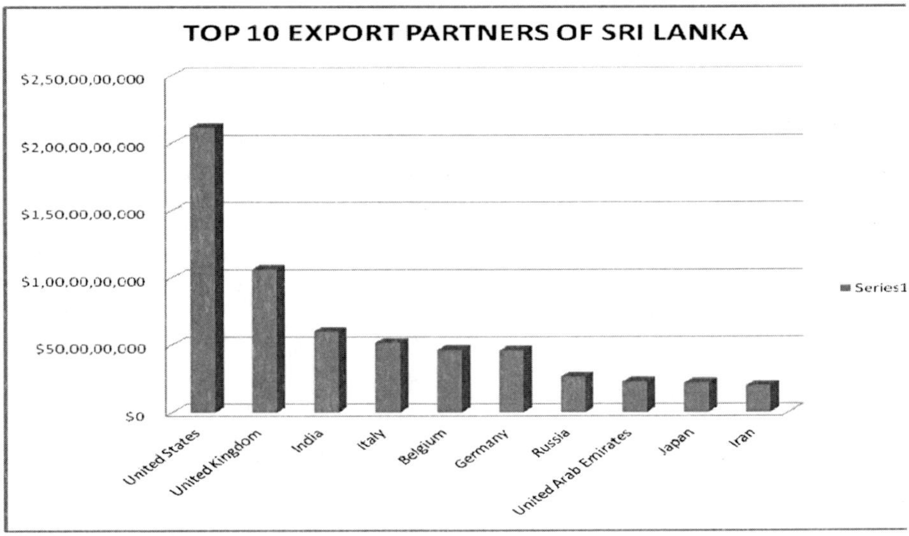

**Source*: Global Edge, Michigan State University.

The above trend in economic relations is a positive sign of good neighbourly relations, which both countries stand to gain from.

Table 1.2

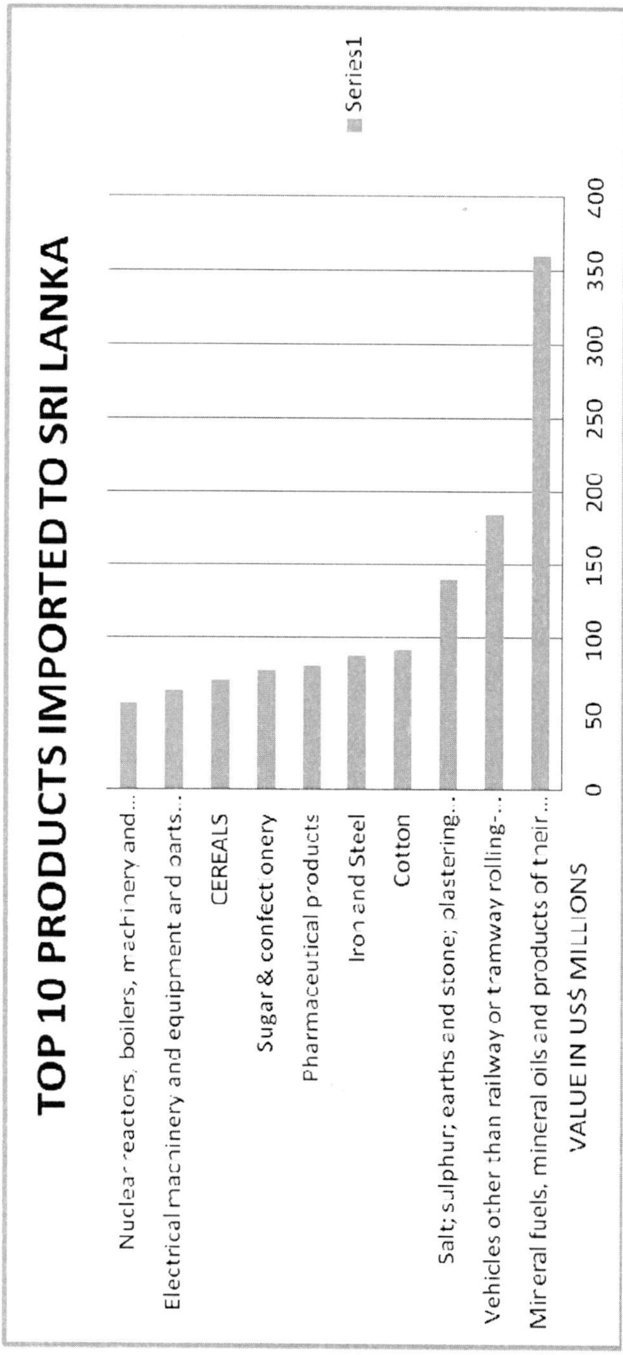

Source: Global Edge, Michigan State University (2014).

Conclusions

The above sketch gives us the picture of the kind of relations that existed between India and Sri Lanka. At the political level, one can note that the Sri Lankan civil war determined the contours of political relations characterised by several ups and downs. The approaches of both countries under different leaderships—President Jayawardene to Mahinda Rajapaksa in Sri Lanka to Prime Minister Indira Gandhi to Manmohan Singh in India – were reactionary and centred on power politics. Both governments were driven by their respective domestic political sentiments which often went against the common interests of establishing peaceful and friendly relations. Although the liberation movement under the LTTE was defeated, yet, the larger problem of Sri Lankan Tamils has not been addressed in terms of reconciling and rehabilitating them. Until this day, thousands of them continue to live in deplorable conditions inviting support from across the border from the regional political parties in Tamil Nadu that are vying to compete with each other to gain political mileage out of it. In fact, it is no exaggeration to say that the regional parties did wield a considerable amount of influence on New Delhi's policy towards the Sri Lankan Tamil issue for a long time. However, with the induction of new Government under Prime Ministership of Narendra Modi with a threshold majority coinciding with the change of guard in Sri Lanka too, the new regime under Maithripala Sirisena brings new hope towards better relations. The age-old outlook too has changed as could be witnessed from the numerous initiatives taken by Modi's government towards solidifying friendly relations with Sri Lanka. Of course, there were precipitating factors that compelled the Modi government to take an independent view bereft of Tamil Nadu. Developments in the Indian Ocean region with China building close ties with the previous Sri Lankan government under Rajapaksa as part of its Maritime Silk Route (MSR) project and seeking port facilities at Hambantota apart from clinching several other economic deals have raised serious concerns for India given the history of animosity between India and China. Notwithstanding the oppositions from India, Sri Lanka's move towards China is nothing but asserting an independent course of action contributing to further strains. In a way, these developments should be viewed as a blessing because it pushed India to adopt a new approach by the new government in India backed up by a successful diplomacy that has now given renewed hopes for a better and stronger bilateral relationship. At the economic level too increase in trade and investments besides several other infrastructural projects have deepened bilateral economic ties. To conclude, blessed with a close geographical proximity and a long history of cultural, religious, and linguistic commonalities the India–Sri Lanka relations have gone beyond other pressing issues. India should continue to engage Sri Lanka and address the issues amicably.

REFERENCES

1. Perera, H R, *Buddhism in Sri Lanka: A Short History*, Kandy: Sri Lanka Buddhist Publication Society, 1988, p. 1.
2. Donation of the Buddha statue has not only been a symbolizing factor to strengthen bilateral religious ties but also a source of competition for both India and China. See Subir Bhaumik, 'China and India use Buddha for regional karma', URL: http://www.aljazeera.com/indepth/features/2013/01/2013171148400871.html (accessed 25th May 2015).
3. Moorthy, Sathiya, 'Sri Lanka and India: its cultural and religious ties', Observer Research Foundation, 2012 URL: http://orfonline.org/cms/sites/orfonline/modules/analysis/AnalysisDetail.html?cmaid=41342&mmacmaid=41343 (accessed 25th May 2015).
4. K.M. De Silva's book presents India has an overwhelmingly dominant, self-aggrandizing regional power, intent on subjugating its weaker neighbours, a tendency that escalated under the imperial "Mrs Gandhi" in 1980s, pp. 8-9.
   De Silva, K.M., *Regional Powers and Small State Security: India and Sri Lanka, 1977-1990*, Washington DC: Woodrow Wilson Centre Press, 1995, p. 388.
5. According to the 2010 Annual Report by the Sri Lankan Ministry of Finance and Planning, there were 295,136 internally displaced people (IDPs) who were unable to go back to their respective homes in the Northern and Eastern provinces. See Ministry of Finance and Planning (2010), *Sri Lanka Annual Report 2010*, Colombo, p. 35. Also, the government claims that a majority of these people were resettled by 2011, there were only 17,785 persons yet to be resettled.
6. See for a good account on this issue, Pattanaik, Smuruti S, 'The Tamil Nadu factor in post-war Sri Lanka: perspectives of Tamils and Muslims", Strategic Analysis, New Delhi, 2014, 38 (5).
7. 'T.N. Assembly Demands Referendum on Eelam', URL: http://www.thehindu.com/news/national/tamil-nadu/tn-assembly-demands-referendum-on-eelam/article4554161.ece (accessed on 18th June 2015).
8. The resolution among others called for an independent international investigation into alleged war crimes and human rights violations in Sri Lanka.
9. Pattanaik, Smuriti S, 'India's abstention in the vote against Sri Lanka at Geneva: likely implications', IDSA, URL: http://www.idsa.in/~idsa/idsacomments/IndiasabstentioninthevoteagainstSriLankaatGeneva_sspattanaik_160414.html (accessed 18th June 2015).
10. Ministry of Finance and Planning, Government of Sri Lanka, 2010, pp. 275-284.
11. Roy, Subhajith (2015), "India takes up fishermen issue after Lanka threat", *The*

Times of India, URL: http://indianexpress.com/article/india/india-others/sushma-swaraj-takes-up-fishermen-issue-with-lanka-pm/ (accessed 19th June 2015).

12. Ibid.
13. 'Prime Minister Modi took up fishermen issue with Sri Lanka, says Sushma Swaraj', *NDTV*, 2015, URL: http://www.ndtv.com/india-news/prime-minister-modi-took-up-fishermen-issue-with-sri-lanka-says-sushma-swaraj-747661 (accessed 19th June 2015).
14. Arrests of some 26 fishermen who were fishing in the high seas by the Sri Lankan Navy were reported as recently as 22nd June 2014.
15. Ibid.
16. 'Electoral victory an opportunity to chart new direction in bilateral | engagement, says President Mukherji to Sri Lankan President', Press Release from the office of President of India, 2015, URL: http://presidentofindia.nic.in/press-release-detail.htm?1365 (accessed on 23 June 2015).
17. Haider, Suhasini, 'Pre-empting China, India inks nuclear pact with Sri Lanka" *The Hindu*, 2015, URL: http://www.thehindu.com/news/national/preempting-china-india-inks-nuclear-pact-with-sri-lanka/article6902874.ece (accessed 23 June 2015)
18. Basu, Nayanima, 'India pushes for comprehensive economic partnership agreement with Sri Lanka', *Business Standard*, 2015, URL: http://www.business-standard.com/article/economy-policy/india-pushes-for-comprehensive-economic-partnership-with-sri-lanka-115031300864_1.html (accessed 22 June 2014).
19. The comprehensive economic partnership agreement which was due to be signed during the SAARC summit in 2008 did not take off until today due to some reservations expressed by the Sri Lankan side. For a good analysis on this see Kelegama, Saman, 'The India–Sri Lanka free trade agreement and the proposed comprehensive economic partnership agreement: A closer look', Asian Development Bank Institute (ADBI), 2014, *Working Paper Series* no 458, Japan.
20. Pattanaik, Smruti S, 'Modi's visit will herald a new chapter in India – Sri Lanka relations", IDSA Comment, URL: http://www.idsa.in/idsacomments/ModisVisitwillHeraldaNewChapter_SPattanaik_120315.html (accessed 22 June 2014).
21. Samaranayake, Nilanthi, 'India's key to Sri Lanka: maritime infrastructure development', URL: http://thediplomat.com/2015/03/indias-key-to-sri-lanka-maritime-infrastructure-development/ (accessed 22 June 2015).
22. Ibid. China's construction projects are much bigger as compared to that of India. It has been involved in port-building projects in Colombo and Hambantota and construction of major highways in cities like Colombo.
23. Basu, Nayanima, 'India pushes for comprehensive economic partnership agreement with Sri Lanka', *Business Standard*, 2015 URL: http://www.business-standard.com/article/economy-policy/india-pushes-for-comprehensive-economic-partnership-with-sri-lanka-115031300864_1.html (accessed 22 June 2014).
24. Department of Commerce (2011), Government of Sri Lanka.

11

China Factor in India's South Asia Policy in Modi Era

D.S. Rajan

Growth and development are the main domestic goals for Prime Minister Narendra Modi's government in India; realising the importance of choosing a foreign policy suitable to achieve them, it has adopted a multi-vectored external approach, which provides for the country's simultaneous relationships with all key international and regional players irrespective of the differences existing among the latter. Symbolising this line have been Modi's hosting of China's Xi Jinping and meeting with Japan's Shinzo Abe as well as his visits to the US, Australia, Seychelles, Mauritius and Sri Lanka. This being so, what cannot be missed is Modi's primacy to the neighbourhood. His vision for South Asia rests on five pillars – trade, investment, assistance and cooperation in every area, contacts between peoples and seamless connectivity;[1] it is natural that in this vision the relationship with the South Asian Association for Regional Cooperation (SAARC) has become crucial. Modi's South Asia policy is vigorously being pushed at action levels. India's leaders have accelerated their contacts with regional powers through exchanging high level visits – Modi to Bhutan, Nepal and Sri Lanka, Foreign Minister Sushma Swaraj to SAARC nations (except Pakistan) and the Indian Foreign Secretary to Bhutan, Bangladesh, Pakistan and Afghanistan.

The People's Republic of China (PRC) had always been a factor in India's South Asia policy; Relevant is the observation made by India's former Prime Minister Dr Manmohan Singh that "there is new assertiveness on the part of China; it will be difficult to say which way it will go and India should be prepared".[2] The China factor will continue to be important for India in the Modi era also. The following reasons given by late Mr B. Raman, a well known analyst is apt – "the PRC is not a South Asian power, but it has acquired a robust South Asian presence through its carefully-cultivated relations with Pakistan, Sri Lanka, the Maldives, Bangladesh and Nepal. It is also not an Indian Ocean power, but it is seeking to acquire a robust Indian Ocean presence through its relations with Myanmar, Bangladesh, Sri Lanka, Maldives, Mauritius & Seychelles. India is a South Asian and Indian Ocean power, but it's South Asian and Indian Ocean influence is being eroded by the increasing inroads of China at the expense of India".[3]

To address the question as to how the China factor influences India's South Asia policy, a pre-requisite will be a clear understanding of Beijing's overall strategic vision at different stages and its linkages to the country's external goals. Such linkages had always been a feature of the PRC's statecraft ever since Chairman Mao Zedong proclaimed the founding of the nation in October 1949, saying that 'China has stood up'. In the Mao Zedong era (1949-76), the strategic vision was consolidation of socialism in China; the matching domestic goals were 'self-reliant development' and the external line was 'leaning to one side', in other words getting the support of socialist allies, for consolidating the Communist party rule at home. Internal priorities underwent a major change in the post-1978 period, with veteran leader Deng Xiaoping made building of 'Socialism with Chinese Characteristics' as a strategic vision; he made reforms and modernisation of the country as domestic goals and chose an open door external line to achieve it.

In the post-Deng period, the then Chinese President Jiang Zemin formulated national policies centring round his theory of "Three Represents", with the objective of making the Chinese Communist Party (CCP) a representative of majority of the people and codified 'three major historic tasks' for China – Modernization, National Reunification and Safeguarding World Peace and Common Development. To accomplish these tasks, he chose an 'Independent Foreign Policy of Peace'. Jiang's successor Hu Jintao brought forth a domestic development model marking a shift in emphasis – from GDP-centric growth to 'balanced development';

to be backed by his own theoretical concept of "Scientific Outlook of Development", of which creation at home of a 'Harmonious Socialist Society' and 'Sustainable development' constituted main elements. Correspondingly, Hu put in place an external strategy based on the idea of a "Harmonious World" aimed at realising a 'win-win' solution in international relations'. The then PRC Premier Wen Jiabao, tracing the links between his country's domestic goals and foreign policy objectives stated, "What China needs for its development first and foremost is an international environment of long term stability and a stable surrounding environment".

For the PRC under President Xi Jinping, 'national rejuvenation' is the strategic vision. For realising it, Xi has set "double century" national goals – (i) building of "moderately prosperous society in all respects" by 2020, the year around 100th anniversary of the CCP's founding, when in all provinces, the average income of the middle class, will reach international standards, China's GDP of 2000 will be quadrupled to approximately $4 trillion with a per capita level of some $3,000. Military mechanisation and major progress in informatisation will be achieved by this time, and (ii) establishment of an 'affluent, strong, civilized, harmonious, socialist modern country' by 2050, the year around the PRC's 100th anniversary, when the annual per capita GDP can reach US$ 40,000, making China one among top 40 countries in the world'. Full military modernisation will also get completed by that time.

In order to achieve the "double century" goals, Xi has chosen a foreign policy course with two pillars – striving for a win–win relationship with external powers and at the same time not compromising on issues concerning territorial sovereignty. The course, with assertiveness as a dominant element, actually began in the middle of 2008; before that Beijing's emphasis in international relations was on 'hiding one's capacities and biding one's time' (veteran leader Deng Xiaoping's famous 24-character maxim of tao guang yang hui). It is an outcome of China's confidence gained through its ability to achieve a sustained growth; also due to its conviction that the country's 'comprehensive national strength' has grown and hence in proportion to that, it should increase its influence over the world. The course is leading to China's display of assertiveness externally, giving rise to fears among neighbours having territorial disputes with the PRC.

Adding further to such fears is China's military modernisation. China's fundamental policy direction is that national defence building should be in the 'service of and subordinated to the country's overall development'. In other words, economic development and military modernisation are to progress hand in hand. China's defence budget for 2014 was to the tune of US$ 132 billion, an increase of 12.2% over previous year. Its military expenditure has had a rapid rise in the past 20 years. The central point is that the development of modernisation in China since 1980s of land, air, naval and missile forces has led to a remarkable expansion in the capabilities of the People's Liberation Army (PLA) for not only defending the country from its soil, but also for operating well beyond its borders to protect PRC's growing global economic and security interests.

To understand the foreign policy of Xi Jinping, especially his approach to neighbours, it would be necessary to look into the reasons behind the PRC's decision, taken at the Central Work Conference on Foreign Relations of the CCP, held in November 2014 to accord top position to relations with neighbours with ties with 'Great Powers' and 'Developing Countries' ranking second and third respectively. The move reflected the PRC's recognition that the periphery including South Asia, is becoming increasingly vital to China's economy, trade and security. Notable in this regard is Xi's stress on the occasion about a Chinese proverb that "close neighbors are better than distant relatives."

Also significant is the concept of ***"Community of Shared Destiny"***, highlighted by Xi at the same conference; it stipulated that "such a community will be based on deep economic integration, but going beyond trade. It will be a vision of a political and security community in which economically integrated countries in the region support and defend one another from outside threats and intruders, as well as manage internal threats together through collaborative and cooperative mechanisms".[4] Xi spoke again on the concept at the Bo Ao Forum (Hainan, 28.3.2015) adding that China, jointly with Asian nations, would build a regional order that is more favourable to Asia and the world. He avoided saying that China would lead such an order; but on the other hand his remarks that "given China's size, it will naturally play a larger role, but without seeking greater monopoly over regional and world affairs", convey a definite meaning. Xi's observations on the occasion that the PRC is ready to sign friendship treaties with neighbouring countries to build trust, are significant. They taken together with his readiness for China-India-Sri Lanka trilateral cooperation to address security concerns in the Indian Ocean region (Xi, Colombo, September 2014) and the PRC's willingness for China-Nepal-India trilateral cooperation (Chinese Foreign Minister Wang Yi, Kathmandu, September 2014) reflect China's new thinking on relations with South Asian nations. In this regard what is looking important is Xi's call for promoting "common, comprehensive, cooperative and sustainable security in Asia", and setting up an "open and inclusive new security architecture in Asia", made at the summit of the Conference on Interaction and Confidence-Building Measures in Asia (CICA), held in Shanghai, in May 2014.

Echoing the vision in the "Community of Shared Destiny" concept are China's two mega proposals for establishing regional connectivity – the Silk Road Economic Belt (SREB) that would be established along the Eurasian land corridor from the Pacific coast to the Baltic Sea, and the 21st century Maritime Silk Road (MSR) connecting Asia and Europe through sea route. Backed by an extensive China-led funding infrastructure, the proposals, as being assessed, could shift the centre of geo-economic power towards Eurasia, and undermine the "Asia Pivot" of the United States and its allies, widely perceived by China as the central plank to contain it. The Chinese expectations from the MSR have come clearly in a document released at the Bo Ao Forum conference, which said that creation of maritime facilities with the PRC's assistance under the MSR will have an obligation for the host country to serve Chinese interests including strategic interests. The document is indeed revelatory of China's intentions to dominate the Asia-Europe region through two proposals. It is very likely that China will develop albeit in a slow manner an increased military presence primarily along the Indian Ocean portions of the MSR. In sum, Xi's concept conveys a firm message to Asian nations - China will use its growing power to reshape economic and security arrangements in the region. India for valid reasons may feel concerned with this. To be noted in this context, is India's policy against giving any blanket endorsement to China's SREB and MSR initiatives and cooperating wherever Indian interests converge with those of China (Indian Foreign Minister Sushma Swaraj, Beijing, February 2015).

Why China now tends to give prominence to economic interests in its foreign policy? According to known Sinologists,[5] it is due to the perception in Xi Jinping's leadership that economic recession is a bigger challenge than external threats. They reveal that a consensus has been reached by the Xi administration on what should be the theoretical foundation of the current major contradictions in the Chinese society. Identifying the "Four Comprehensives" concept introduced by Xi Jinping in December 2014 ("comprehensively, build a moderately prosperous society, strengthen reforms, establish rule of law and set up party that have defined") as such foundation, they have observed that the leader, unlike his predecessors, seems to have realised that the central task of development can be achieved only if changes could be brought into the structure of international economic and political order. Also according to them, President Xi Jinping has redefined and expanded the function of Chinese diplomacy and that he will attempt to alter some of the foreign policy processes and power relationship that have defined the political, military, and economic environment in the Asia-Pacific region.[6]

One of the requirements for China's modernisation has been a stable neighbourhood, especially South Asia. The same continues in Xi Jinping's China. There are also other determinants of his South Asia policy. They include neutralising the perceived US strategy to contain China with support of regional nations, developing economies of China's border areas, cooperating with South Asian countries in exploitation of much needed energy resources, protecting oil transport security in the Indian Ocean, getting support to 'One China' policy and last but not least securing cooperation from the nations in the region in the matter of meeting terrorism – a major threat to China's south-western border from outside.

As it looks now, the Xi regime may in principle not dilute its hitherto followed assertive neighbourhood approach, but its economic interests-based external line may demand the country showing some moderation at action levels, for e.g. China's willingness to talk with ASEAN on the code of conduct in the South China Sea. This would be welcome news for China's neighbours involved in territorial disputes with the PRC. This being the general situation, the thrust of Xi Jinping's South Asia policy, needs a mention. As seen by China analysts, that is to 'maintain a strategic balance' in that region.[7] Xi is likely to concentrate on strengthening 'multidimensional cooperation' with countries in South Asia. In it, Beijing unmistakably seems to be giving a prominent space to India. As a result of Xi's visit to India in September 2014, prospects for bilateral cooperation in new areas including industrial investment, infrastructure development, energy conservation and environment protection have increased. Steps towards rebalancing bilateral trade and addressing the existing structural imbalance in trade are now being undertaken by them. Of particular significance, is the PRC's willingness to establish two industrial parks in India, one in Gujarat and one in Maharashtra and to invest US$20 billion in the next 5 years in various industrial and infrastructure development projects in India. China is looking for a more flexible and comprehensive policy to accommodate the present situation, and to some extent, respond to the related arguments of China as a threat in the region. India's fears are over being encircled by a Chinese 'string of pearls' and losing control of the Indian Ocean.

In a strategic sense, the background to Xi's India policy is to be noted. Beijing's stabilisation of ties with New Delhi has gained momentum through signing important agreements with India like the Strategic and Cooperative Partnership for Peace and Prosperity and Political Parameters and Guiding Principles for Settlement of the Boundary Question (2005), 'Shared Vision for the 21st Century (2008) and the Border Defence agreement (2013). China has stopped treating India as a threat to it and views that Sino-Indian ties have attained a global character. China seems to realise that cooperation with India is essential for it in tackling global issues like the WTO, climate change, global financial system reform and revamping of UN Security Council. It can be seen without difficulty that congruence, to a good degree, of policy interests among China and India has emerged over the years; under its impact, in general, the comfort level in their relations has been increasing.

The PRC in fact began to stress on a 'balanced' South Asia policy in the end-seventies, in pursuance of the conceived pre-requisite to have a 'peaceful periphery' conducive to its modernisation. Under it, the PRC had modified its pro-Pakistan stand so far kept on Kashmir issue, with the state-controlled media dropping references to 'India-occupied Kashmir' and using instead the terms 'India-controlled Kashmir' and 'Pakistan-controlled Kashmir'. In December 1996, the then Chinese President Jiang Zemin favored New Delhi–Islamabad 'consultations and negotiations' on the Kashmir issue, during his speech to the Pakistan Senate. During the Kargil conflict in 1999, China refrained from taking sides and adopted a neutral position. China's oft-repeated stand since this time has been that the Kashmir issue is one 'left over by history' and that 'India and Pakistan should properly solve the problem through dialogue and negotiations'. Beijing no longer makes references to 'self-determination' for the Kashmiri people and does not consider the 'Kashmiri people' as a third party to the dispute.

Nevertheless, worrisome to India however is that China under Xi Jinping is pursuing the railway projects of the previous government, designed to link Pakistan and China via Pakistan Occupied Kashmir (POK) where Chinese troops are reportedly deployed ostensibly for construction work. The reported infrastructure projects undertaken by the Chinese military and nuclear establishments in Pakistan Occupied Gilgit-Baltistan region, may become strategically important to the Chinese army in the event of another conflict with India; in particular, the Karakoram Highway could be useful for China as an overland route for moving missiles and spare parts to Pakistan. China-Pakistan Economic Corridor coming under Xi Jinping's Silk Road initiative passes through Pakistan Occupied Kashmir. Also, there appears to be a deeper meaning to the continuing issue of stapled visas by Beijing to Indians from Kashmir. This may mark a nuanced Chinese position on Kashmir implying a dilution of China's past stand of accepting Kashmir as a de facto part of India, while at the same time treating POK including Gilgit-Baltistan region as de facto and de jure parts of Pakistan. Is China's stand a quid pro quo for Pakistan's help to Beijing in fighting against Uighur separatism in Xinjiang? Is Beijing developing future options for questioning India's locus standi to negotiate with China on the territory in Ladakh ceded by Pakistan to the PRC? The remarks of the then Indian Prime Minister that China "could use India's soft underbelly of Kashmir to keep India in low level equilibrium",[8] demonstrate how serious these questions are.

What has been said above shows that the Xi Jinping regime in China, despite putting economic interests first in its foreign policy including on South Asia, may not give up its assertiveness on key issues – Sino-Indian border, Tibet and Sino-Pak nexus. The PRC is becoming more vociferous in claiming India's Arunachal Pradesh as part of its 'Southern Tibet' for e.g. its objection to the Indian Prime Minister's visit to Arunachal Pradesh. It is suspecting India's position on the Dalai Lama in spite of New Delhi's assurances on this count and keeping the talks between Dharamsala and Beijing deadlocked. It is further strengthening strategic ties with Pakistan.

Both China and Pakistan are repeatedly laying stress on the relevance to bilateral ties of their peace treaty signed in 2005, unique in South Asia, providing for mutual support in protecting each other's national sovereignty and integrity; this treaty is being mentioned in several China-Pakistan joint statements. For China, the vital sea route for its energy import from the Middle East has become more important from the point of view of the South Asian situation. It is natural for India to watch for the strategic significance of China's naval modernisation and its increasing focus on the Indian Ocean. In this context, the real meaning of the bold views, but without official contradiction, expressed by influential military and strategic experts in China on setting up its overseas naval bases to protect the country's energy supply routes, should be a matter of concern for India; Indian fears over the future military potentials of China's port projects in India's neighbourhood, like Gwadar (Pakistan), Hambantota (Sri Lanka), Sittwe (Myanmar) and Chittagong (Bangladesh) are core concerns of India's security.

Xi Jinping administration is projecting China's economic power into countries in India's neighbourhood and thereby gaining capabilities to influence these countries strategically. This is putting India under compulsion to suitably challenge China. China has become the largest investor in Sri Lanka. During Xi's recent visit to Colombo, Sri Lanka and China reached 27 agreements, including one to start negotiations on a free-trade agreement. China has several large-scale, ongoing projects in Bangladesh which include deep seaports in Chittagong and Sonadia Island. China also has plans to build a road and rail link through Myanmar to connect the Chinese city of Kunming to Chittagong. China has invested heavily in the Nepalese energy and transportation sectors, including a US$ 1.6 billion hydropower plant and a US$ 1.9 billion railroad project to connect Lhasa to Kathmandu. Other transportation projects include the Pokhara Regional International Airport, a number of roads, bridges and container depots. China has pledged to vastly increase its investment in Pakistan's economy and infrastructure sector. Among other initiatives, China has been helping develop Pakistan's infrastructure sector through the construction of power plants, roads and communication nodes. China is the largest investor in Pakistan's Gwadar Deep Sea Port, and Prime Minister Nawaz Sharif is working towards the China-Pakistan Economic Corridor plan, having already approved a list of early projects including power, roads, railways, the Gwadar port, and energy projects, totalling roughly US$ 35 billion. China and Pakistan are negotiating whether to put their energy projects on a fast track in the China-Pakistan Economic Corridor.

India may have to deal with the Chinese enthusiasm to enter the SAARC on the basis of mutual advantage. Chinese scholars believe[9] that combined, the economic integration of the PRC and SAARC will create a huge market with 2.8 billion people, which will bring a new force for economic development to China, South Asia and the whole world. The PRC wants to establish a China–SAARC free trade area. The scholars also think that India pays close attention to China's economic relations with other South Asian countries under the belief that they are aimed at Chinese encirclement of India. They accuse India as interfering in other South Asian countries' economic agreements with China, both openly and covertly. India's contradictions with other South Asian countries will not disappear overnight, unless India abandons its ambition to play the role of "big brother" in South Asia. Furthermore, India's economic development over the past two decades has not produced substantial spillover effects for its neighbours. The scholars further say that SAARC is now in need of external forces to help drive its development and integration. Whether India likes it or not, it will be unable to prevent other SAARC countries from turning to China for financial support.

In conclusion, it can be said that India under Modi, will have both opportunities and challenges in the South Asia policy of China under Xi Jinping. India can work towards capitalising on the economic opportunities which may arise in South Asia as Xi promotes his 'shared destiny' concept to connect the region, especially through channelling funds through the China-led Asia Infrastructure Investment Bank (AIIB). India is a member of the AIIB. In a strategic sense, however, India should be prepared to face challenges as Xi's policy appears to aim at establishing a new Asian order in which China will play a big, if not leading, role. Hypothetically speaking, the neighbours of the PRC including India which want to benefit from close economic ties with China, but at the same time feel compulsions to worry about Beijing's aggressive push of its territorial claims, will feel relieved if Xi Jinping's China, under its economic interests-driven foreign policy, tones down its assertiveness abroad at action levels. In reality however the situation is different; consider the creation of artificial islands in South China Sea by China with an eye on gaining strategic superiority vis-à-vis other claimants. This being so, undoubtedly one has to wait further for a full picture; much would depend on the nature of future domestic and foreign policy developments in China. China's readiness to sign friendship treaties with its neighbours has been a notable development with major implications for future prospects for the regional geopolitics. In such circumstances, it would be beneficial for India to probe the Chinese new foreign policy thinking including on South Asia, utilising the opportunity of the impending visit to Beijing by its Prime Minister.

REFERENCES

1. Narendra Modi (2014), Speech delivered on November 2014 at SAARC summit, Kathmandu: Nepal.
2. Indian PM Singh Says 'China Would Like Foothold in South Asia' URL: http://www.2point6billion.com/news/2010/09/07/indian-pm-singh-says-%E2%80%98china-would-like-foothold-in-south-asia%E2%80%99-7037.html#sthash.o4G2KI2c.dpuf
3. Raman, B. (2010), "Chinese Inroads into Sri Lanka", URL: http://www.outlookindia.com/article/ChineseInroads-Into-Sri-Lanka/265026
4. "China *Overhauls Diplomacy* to Consolidate Regional Leadership, Outline Strategy for Superpower Ascent", *China Brief* Volume 14, issue 24, 19.12.2014
5. Health, Timothy (2015), " Xi's Bold Foreign Policy Agenda – Beijing's Pursuit of Global Influence and Growing Risk of Sino-US Rivalry", China Brief, URL: http://www.jamestown.org/programs/chinabrief/single/?tx_ttnews[tt_news]=43674&tx_ ttnews[backPid]=25&cHash=071fa8755bd5400d7292613f67
6. Swaine, Michael D. (2015), *China Leadership Monitor,* " Xi Jinping's Address to the Central Conference on Work Relating to Foreign Affairs: Assessing and Advancing Major Power Diplomacy with Chinese Characteristics", URL: http://www.hoover.org/publications/china-leadership-monitor.
7. "Pakistan, China agree on maintaining strategic balance in S Asia" covering the visit to Pakistan by Chinese Foreign Minister Wang Yi, *Daily Times,* February 14, 2015.
8. Remarks made by Dr Manmohan Singh, *Times of India*: Chennai, October 7, 2010.
9. Zongyi, Liu (2014), "China's Economic Relations with SAARC: Prospects and Hurdles", lecture delivered on December 1, 2014 at China Institute of International Studies: Beijing.

12

India in South Asia: Challenges and Opportunities

*Mahendra P. Lama**

Historical narratives and discourse have partly dominated India's foreign policy design, construction and practices. For decades together, the non-alignment movement remained as one of the major planks of India's global leadership among the developing and newly decolonised countries. This movement became a widely accepted forum for the developing countries mainly because of the common cause these countries together propounded. This led to many powerful conglomerations like the Group of 77 and also the setting up of UNCTAD in the UN. These three institutions later became the vanguard of negotiations with the North on critical issues like stability of commodity prices, transfer of technology, development assistance to developing countries and also opening of markets and several other politico-strategic issues. The North was literally forced to agree on the appointment of two commissions, the Pearson Committee in 1969 and Brandt Commission in 1980, both of which strongly supported the cause of the global South. This is how the New International Economic Order resolution was passed by the UN in 1974.

---

*Transcript from Prof. Mahendra P Lama's lecture delivered at a national seminar organised by the UGC Centre for Southern Asia Studies, Pondicherry University on "Neighbourhood Initiatives of Modi Government: Challenges and Road Ahead" held on April 20-22, 2015.

In all these North–South negotiations a crucial issue has been the secular decline in primary commodity prices thereby, very deeply and adversely affecting the terms of trade of developing countries. Raul Previsch and Hans Singer empirically demonstrated how developing countries were made to export primary commodities, basically raw materials like bauxite, iron ore, cotton, copper, wool, etc., and how these commodities were converted into the final products and re-exported back to developing countries at a price many times higher than the raw materials. In the process, the cream of development was usurped by the developed countries as they had the advantage of having technology, capital, industrial ventures and control over the policies that govern the world trading and investment system.

It is memorable that besides the political regimes, our international negotiators and intellectual leaders like Sukhomoy Chakrovorthy, G. Prathasarathy, L.K. Jha, K.B. Lall, Nikhil Chakravarty, Muchkund Dubey and others vehemently fought against such discriminatory practices. Ultimately, the North–South Negotiations failed in the early 1980s as the North suffered from the withdrawal and fatigue syndrome which then led to what we call South–South Cooperation primarily in the form of Economic Cooperation among Developing Countries (ECDC).

Look at the situation today; India has again become the victim of the same trend and practice. However the theatre of operation is not global; it is now regional, and the critical actor in this intriguing drama are not the developed market economies, but our own neighbour, China. It is China which despite being a developing country, consistently kept itself outside the NAM and other conglomerations of the South–South that highlighted these issues. The time is not immediate post-colonial situation; it is a post-cold war situation under which means, market, instrumentalities and even the comparative advantages are strikingly similar. However, the victim, India, which consistently fought against such a trend for full four decades and today doesn't even express concerns, has remained the same and is keeping silence. India's trade with China started steadily increasing in the 1990s and reached a volume of almost a billion from a mere 40 million in 1990. India has a huge trade deficit. In 2013–2014, India's exports to China were $ 14.8 billion and imports were a hefty $ 51 billion with a trade deficit of over $ 36 billion. The terms of trade have been blatantly and conspicuously against India. More seriously, despite being a manufacturing hub, Indian exports to China are in overwhelmingly primary commodities i.e. raw or semi-raw materials, but our imports are finished products like telecom equipment, electrical machinery, computer and mobile hardware. Unlike during the four decades of the 1950s to the 1980s, we have literally no stand on this very ominous trend and practice; no voice has been raised and no measures are being taken to correct the situation. This has already happened for 15 years now. We remain a silent victim. China has done this to other developing regions including Africa, Central and South Asia and Middle-East Asia. This is a quiet intrusion rather invasion on the natural endowments.

This is where Prime Minister Modi's initiative on "Make in India" stands to be critical. This is because it is at the heart of using your own raw materials for your own manufacturing and other production bases and enjoying the huge value added benefits that emanate from regional and global markets. This would also restrict literally unbridled exports of raw materials and inspire research and development (R&D) activities in the country. This is what the Chinese did. It used its comparative advantage of raw materials and relatively cheaper labour by bringing most of the top multinationals from Japan, Europe and US to Guangdong, Fujian, Shanghai, Zhejiang, Jiangsu, Shandong and Liaoning provinces of China in the form of small and medium enterprises (SMEs) and auxiliary units. This is why we have National Panasonic to Sony and GE to cosmetics made in China.

Therefore, the present Government led by PM Modi has a formidable challenge firstly to go back to history, check why India fought against such a trend and how it mobilised the global South for this purpose and correct these distortionary and discriminatory practices. Can "Make in India" campaign be globalised fitting it into other developing countries' perspectives? Can India lead from the front? Could India do it alone or have a newer platform to do so? This is a big question to be addressed.

Many significant developments are taking place around India that will have transformational changes in the geopolitics and socio-economic structures in this region and other connecting regions of India. Let me mention just one such Herculean deviation and historic departure quietly advocated yet so quickly propagated by China i.e. the "Silk Road Economic Belt and 21st century Maritime Silk Road also known as the Belt and Road project". The vision document of China on this initiative issued on March 28, 2015 mentions:

> "The Belt and Road Initiative aims to promote the connectivity of Asian, European and African continents and their adjacent seas, establish and strengthen partnerships among the countries along the Belt and Road, set up all-dimensional, multi-tiered and composite connectivity networks, and realize diversified, independent, balanced and sustainable development in these countries. The connectivity projects of the initiatives will help align and coordinate the development strategies of the countries along the belt and road, tap market potential in this region, promote investment and consumption, create demands and job opportunities, enhance people to people contact and cultural exchanges, and mutual learning among the peoples of the relevant countries, and enable them to understand, trust and respect each other and live in harmony, peace and prosperity" and "it is open to all countries and international and regional organizations for engagement, so that the results of the concerted efforts will benefit wider areas".

The "Silk Road Spirit" propagated, communicated and practiced between the East and West, was a clear enunciation of what China's grand thinking, overarching programmes and staggering projects are going to be in the next few decades in its quest to be a global leader and in the promotion of "peace and cooperation, openness and inclusiveness, mutual learning and mutual benefit". This is further consolidation of Deng Xiaoping's "comprehensive periphery policy" and also integrated regional policy also known as "Zhoubian Zhengce" (peripheral policy) and neighbourhood policy is also known as "Mulin Zhengce". The centrality of China in this far-reaching project was assiduously propagated by Xi Jinping and his team; it is inevitable and insurmountable.

This document brings in five issues of significance to India. Firstly, the Chinese have already tested the ground quietly, effectively and pragmatically across the region from the South, South-East, Central and Middle East to Europe and beyond in terms of what they call 'connectivity' and 'cooperation initiatives. "Gwadar port", "Lhasa–Kathmandu Railway Line", Shigatshe–Nathula railway line are just few examples.

Secondly, they are quite clear and partly ready with regard to the strategies to be followed and the institutions to be built in order to carry out these projects.

Thirdly, they also have the blue print of major projects already in their store and have also made grounds for their implementation in consultation with the respective concerned countries and their governments.

Fourthly, they would have already made basic calculations on the geopolitics, political economy, financial coasts and economic benefits of these projects broadly in areas like strategic gains, economic benefits, sustainability features including access to the connecting countries' resources and finally, they are also clear as to the setting up of Special Purpose Vehicles (SPVs) like the Asian Infrastructure Investment Bank (AIIB) and have even proposed the Silk Road Bank in orderly to swiftly, deftly and smoothly implement and operationalise these projects. The China-Pakistan Economic Corridor, a plan for $ 46 billion network of roads, railways and energy projects linking Pakistan's deepwater Gwadar port on the Arabian Sea with China's far-western Xinjiang region is one example. It would shorten the route for China's energy imports by passing the straits of Malacca between Malaysia and Indonesia, a bottleneck at risk of blockade in wartime.

The philosophy and finer nuances are couched in sophisticated yet popular and accommodative expressions like five principles of peaceful coexistence, inclusiveness, cooperation, mutual benefits, and 'give full play to the wisdom and creativity, strengths and potentials of all parties'.

Depending upon the nature, orientation and scale of India's engagement in the 'Belt and Road' project, as this concept and its operationalisation unfolds over the next few years, there will be significant opportunities and gains for India too. However, foreseeable implications for India from the neighbourhood perspectives are at this juncture are broadly threefold. Firstly, this will be China's most effective entry, penetrative practices and durable presence into the geographies, societies and economies of this region. It could inject newer varieties of vulnerabilities into India's neighbourhood.

Secondly, it could change the entire matrices of India's bilateral relations with the neighbouring countries and could trigger a "new regionalism" exclusively based on connectivity and communication and related openness of geographies and people. This could even render regional organisations like the SAARC ineffective.

And thirdly, the Indian economy's identity and exclusivity could be jeopardised and sub-merged into the conundrum of hugely connected geographies and emerging socio-economic complexities. This will happen when neighbouring countries permit penetrations into China to reach India's own crucial peripheries and borderlands.

This is where one finds serious and formidable challenges before the Government led by Prime Minister Modi. There are choices of ignoring it, showing indifferences, reacting to it and pro-acting and of course, redesigning and restructuring India's traditional postures and policies into the grand vision and overarching plan that ill-locate and reposition India's regional and global presence and significance. The conventional posture of always thinking about war but talking about peace could no longer be relevant in the emerging situations in India's neighbourhood. More seriously, long-practiced policies of instrumentalism and micro-management techniques need to be instantly reconsidered and discarded.

In this context, one must recall that the previous Government of UPA had started moving in this direction. An example is the India–Bangladesh deals. The unilateral removal of trade restrictions to all the LDCs under SAFTA; three major power deals like Behrampur– Bheramara transmission line, sale of 500 MW power through national grid interconnection of India and 1400 MW Khulna Thermal project and Teesta Agreements and Land Border Agreements with Bangladesh are few of the examples. This was definitely a major deviation from the same Government's policies of dealing with Bangladesh with high-handness and one-upmanship in 2005, and in the process losing the Myanmar-Bangladesh-India gas pipeline and India's transit to the North-east through Bangladesh.

All these call for four crucial strategic considerations in India's neighbourhood policies.

Firstly, India should act really like the leader, a big country with an inclusive heart. Prime Minister Modi must be portrayed as a strong custodian of regionalism-based development like what was Lee Kaun for ASEAN, Robert Mugabe and Julius Nyrere in SADC and Mitterrand and Kohl for EU.

Secondly, India must draw a new vision about its neighbouhood policies. Could we think of a Grand Himalayan Policy that will link Kolkata and eastern regions of India with Inner and Central Asia through the Tibetan Autonomous Region and Sichuan province in China with a corridor named as the Grand Himalayan Corridor (GHC)? Could we similarly adopt the Act East Policy in a time-bound manner with a focus on the completion of projects with Myanmar, trilateral highways with Myanmar and Thailand and speedy implementation of the proposed BCIM corridor? Could we make India the energy hub of South Asia by operationalising the concept of 'Energy Ring' as propounded by Prime Minister Atal Bihari Vajpayee in the Islamabad Summit (12th) in 2004 and by operationalising the long-standing energy projects involving Pakistan, Afghanistan and the Central Asian and West Asian countries, linking this to the SAARC–ASEAN power grid and gas pipeline? Could we have a multimodal land bridge between the South Indian states and Sri Lanka? All these would supplement and complement what China's 'Belt and Road Projects promote through the Gwadar–Xinjiang region and the Nepal–Tibet Corridor.

Thirdly, the challenge is to re-organise and relocate borders as borderlands where there are an intrinsic inter-play of natural resources, culture, societies, trade and commerce, tourism, water, towers, technology, roads and communications. The moment we do this we tend to make borders softer and interactive. This makes economic integration and people-to-people contacts much more pacific. Unfortunately, the colonial legacy made us think of a border purely as a geometric line, roughly a *Laxman rekha*, and we increasingly became what we proverbially call *lakir ka fakir*. In the process two very countervailing situations emerged. Firstly, the borders became only a source of national security threat and have to be protected by the security forces alone. And secondly, the entire historical emergence of the borderland which actually determined the cultural ecology, political economy and biodiversity and environmental flows of this subcontinent has been conveniently sidetracked and systematically dismantled. Borders thus became a bastion of orthodox military thinking and human security dynamics were utterly neglected.

This author's own experience in the reopening of the once versatile Nathu La trade route between Sikkim and TAR after 44 years in 2006 has partly convinced him about the criticality of reconnecting with the borderlands. Today, the route is being used for Kailash Manasarovar pilgrimage yatra.

The more the local integration, the softer become the border. When the borderlands become more vibrant, physical borders become a little secondary. Once the border becomes softer, orthodox military-centric treatment of borders actually transforms into opportunities galore which in turn could lead to resolutions of many political imbroglios.

And finally, could we really redesign and reallocate the role of our bordering constituent states in the entire process of this new grand architecture? We have 15,106 km of land border running through 94 districts in 17 states with a population of over 40 million. Could we allow these federal units in the periphery with flexibility, autonomy and a pivotal role in the conceptualising, designing and implementation of these projects? How do we build institutions and human capacities in these states, how do we blend the international financing institutions and global construction agencies in these states? The Palatana gas-based power project in Tripura is an example of how a federal unit in the North Eastern Region (NER) of India could convert a project of national interest into a state project with strong cross-border linkage with Bangladesh. Though there is no legal agreement to use the Bangladeshi territory for transporting goods and services to the North-east region of India, Tripura was quietly given the facilities to transport all the machineries and goods through Chittagong ports and other land routes in Bangladesh that has a stake in the import from the project. This is the first project in the NER being carried out with a SPV by three partners viz., NTPC, ILFS and Tripura Government.

More than a decade ago, the *Economist* magazine published a photograph where India was shown as a tiger inside the cage. It, in a way, conveyed that if the cage is opened and the tiger comes out, it could do wonders, make unbelievable moves and bring unparallel achievements. Interestingly, today the cage is open but the tiger does not want to come out. Prime Minister Modi's team must come out of the cage and act and behave like a free tiger that would bring brightness, life, prosperity, cooperation, peace and stability both within the country and to the neighbourhood.

Index